Unknown Heroes

A Strange Story
of a
Lost Company of Marines

George W. Sciple

Williams & Company, Publishers
Savannah, Georgia

Second Edition

Manufactured in the United States of America

ISBN 1-878853-78-3
Copyright©2003, 2006
by George W. Sciple

Williams & Company, Publishers
1317 Pine Ridge Drive
Savannah, Georgia 31406

Acknowledgements

THIS WORK COULD not have been brought to completion without the perseverance, skill, and patience of Marjorie McKee Sciple. Marjorie S. Harris has been of great help in preparation of the manuscript. I thank her as well.

Were it not for our men's courage, skill, and capacity to persist in their duty under appalling conditions of privation, I would not be here to tell these stories.

Table of Contents

Foreword

FOR YEARS I have read supposedly authentic accounts of combat experiences of United States military people and organizations. Some of the authors, screenwriters, and others have seemed not to have any grasp whatsoever of what real living and wartime fighting is. Others are concerned with what the author's beliefs are concerning the grand strategies of commanders and national leaders, most or all of whom they apparently have known only by reputation.

The accounts by these people are so far from my own experience that I want to tell those of you who read these stories what a little-known bit of the fighting in the Pacific in World War II was really like. The stories are personal accounts of my own: raw, bloody, grim, terrible, funny and wonderful all at the same time. In them I will tell you over and over again about being lost. Perhaps then, out of your own experience of being lost, you will have some grasp of how utterly lost we were.

General Robert E. Lee once said that we need constantly to be reminded of how awful war is lest we come to love it. May these stories be such a reminder.

—George W. Sciple

Introduction

WE WERE LOST in the Pacific area in World War II. I'll tell you how we got lost and how it was being lost. I'll do this with several more or less chronologically arranged short stories. These will let you know how the living, and dying, was in a series of combat and reconnaissance operations. There may be no other written record of some of these.

We were a company of somewhat fewer than 130 men. Our commanding officer was a captain. Lt. Gaebe was a platoon leader. I was the company executive officer and vehicle maintenance officer. We had three platoon leaders and a full roster of non-commissioned officers, headed by our first sergeant and our gunnery sergeant.

We were a "Landing Vehicle, Tracked (LVT)" outfit. The mission of LVTs early in the war was to carry munitions and supplies from our ships through the sea, over the reef, across the beach and up to the riflemen, mortar platoons and artillery outfits engaging the Japanese. This seemed to me to be relatively cushy duty with a far lesser chance of getting your ass blown off than what was soon to come. I reveled in it during our training at Camp Lejeune and Camp Pendleton. While we were at Camp Pendleton and developing procedures for loading and unloading in the open sea from the interior of LSTs (Landing Ships, Tank), our mission suddenly changed. We were now ordered to land the first waves of assaults, bringing men already loaded into LVTs from ships directly to the beach. Cushy duty suddenly developed into something else indeed. Our men were superb, real marines. They accepted this grim task simply as their duty. There was apprehension at the prospect of heavy, heavy casualties, but no whining.

LVTs were strange, ungainly things, officially termed Amphibian Tractors. Clumsy, slow, awkward, short-lived, and requiring constant maintenance, they had one immense advantage. They could travel in water and on land. They really were amphibians.

Each was made of thin steel to reduce weight and allow the pontoon-like hull to float. They had a rear-mounted, seven-cylinder, radial, air-cooled, 250-horsepower engine. A large clutch was fitted within a circular, many-bladed cooling fan. There was a long, waist-high, shielded drive shaft down the middle of an open, box-like cargo compartment. The shaft passed into a small, forward driver's compartment which housed a great, heavy transmission, differential and final drive unit. These transmitted power via axles through the hull to toothed sprockets which drove steel tracks on each side of the hull.

The vehicle was steered by two large, heavy hand levers which worked brakes within the differential. Pulling one brake lever would slow the speed of the sprocket on one side of the vehicle and allow the other track to turn faster, thus redirecting the course of the vehicle toward the slow-track side. This arrangement operated on land as well as in the water. The tracks had two-inch tall, W-shaped, steel, cuplike cleats every few inches. These cleats scooped water and drove the LVT through the sea, as well as giving added traction on land. We could travel, at a maximum and in a new vehicle, a bit over six knots in the water and about twice that on land.

Each LVT was about twenty feet long, seven feet high, and weighed about 33,000 pounds. A small cab was mounted forward near the bow. It housed the driver and a co-driver, as well as the great transmission, differential and final drive units. It took a small man both hands and arms to shift speeds in the transmission. The shift lever was close to the diameter of the driver's wrist and about 2.5 feet long. We had five forward gear ratios and one reverse. When absolutely brand new and on a smooth, firm, level beach, we could run in fourth gear. I never saw one that could run in fifth gear. In the water, we had to run in first, second or third gear. Even new, we could not use fourth gear in the water, except in the most unusual circumstances. Our engine usually had to be operated at between 1800 and 2250 rpm. We had an automatic revolution-limiter which would not allow operation at over 2250 rpm. The engine would self-destruct at much above 2250 rpm. There was an electric starter for the engine. We used 60-weight engine oil for lubrication and gasoline for fuel.

Vibration from the engine, transmission, final drive units, sprockets, and tracks was extreme. When we had an inch or two of water on the steel deck inside the open cargo compartment and were operating at full engine speed in third gear in the water, we would routinely have vibration-induced spray rising to our waists or higher, keeping us soaked with sea water. Many of our men had deafness and problems maintaining balance after long periods of running at full speed in water.

Maintenance of the vehicles was exceptionally time consuming. The W-shaped cleats, for instance, were fixed to the steel tracks with three-quarter inch head bolts. The cleats would loosen after an hour or so of running and sling off, or worse, sling sideways and drag along the thin metal of the hull. The tracks themselves had to be adjusted frequently for correct tension. Throwing a track while at sea was a potential catastrophe, since it could not be refitted. The LVT could then make no progress with only one track and would simply turn in circles.

Our men did a fine job of keeping these demanding machines running. Their lives depended on their doing so.

We were originally a part of an LVT battalion consisting of three companies and a headquarters company. The battalion was commanded by a lieutenant colonel. He had a major as his executive officer. The battalion was a part of a reinforced marine division. In the landing in the Marshall Islands, we were attached to a marine division. Later, in the landing at Guam, we were attached to the First Provisional Marine Brigade. It was composed of the Raider Regiment and the 22nd Marine Regiment. A brigadier general was in command.

We, in our Lost Company, were ordered back and forth so frequently that we could hardly keep up with the outfits we were operating with. In turn, the senior officers of the organizations we were working with did not even have us on their personnel rosters. Our men, as far as I am aware, never received the unit commendation medals awarded to the organizations with which we operated.

We were, from an administrative standpoint, nonentities. Not only were we lost; we failed to exist.

Our first operation was the attack on the Marshall Islands. We combat-loaded in San Diego for the 4000-5000 mile voyage to the Marshall Islands. We were to proceed in convoy to the Hawaiian Islands, join with our destroyers, cruisers, carriers and battleships there, then proceed to Kwajalein Atoll in the Marshalls. A minor problem developed with our convoy, however. The convoy's lead navigator made a computation error. We missed the entire Hawaiian Islands by several hundred miles, ending up nearly running aground at French Frigate Shoals. We had to turn about and sail back to the Hawaiian Islands. This delayed the whole operation and forced us to live in miserable, jam-packed, cramped conditions for three weeks before we could go into what we knew was going to be a grim fight.

I will start with stories about happenings in the Kwajalein Atoll operation and then go on to stories of our landing
to recapture Guam in the Marianas Islands. Though out of
temporal sequence, I will then tell you about our great adventure in the reconnaissance through the Ralik, or western,
chain of the Marshalls. I will finish with a final story which
ends our overseas duty.

Figure 1. Side view of an LVT

Figure 2. Front view of an LVT

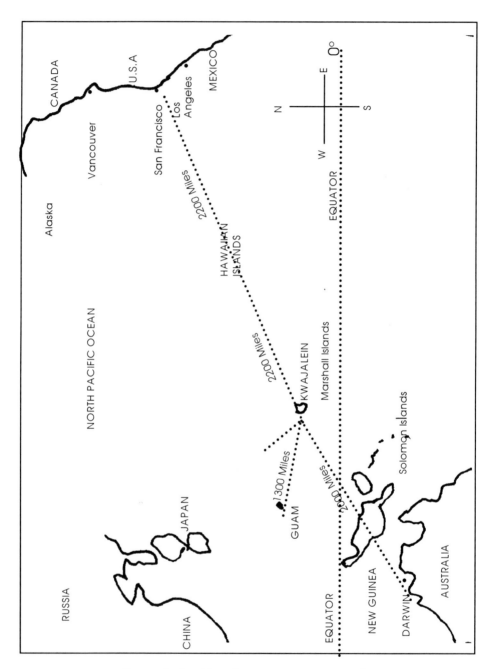

Figure 3. Pacific. (Drawing not to scale)

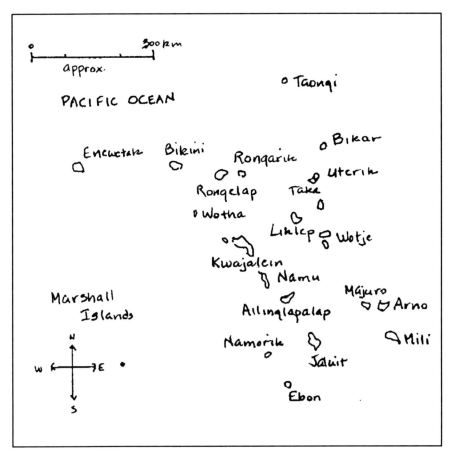

Figure 4. Marshall Islands

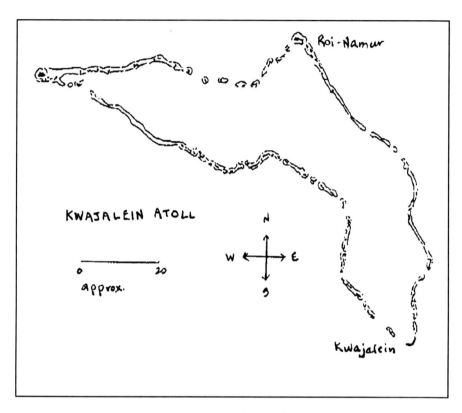

Figure 5. Kwajalein Atoll

Lost

I'LL TELL YOU how we got lost. We were ordered to occupy a tiny islet far down the reef at Kwajalein Atoll after our marine division troops took the north end of the atoll from the Japanese in a desperate three-day fire fight.

There was fierce fighting until our people could kill the approximately four thousand Japs defending the two islands of Roi and Namur at the north end of the Kwajalein reef.

During the fighting, we had many of our company's tracked, amphibian assault vehicles, called LVTs, shot up, wrecked and damaged. These were lying on the lagoon side of the reef, where they had been hit when we had carried in the first waves of troops.

Our support ships could not land supplies on the open ocean side of the island because of the immense waves that surged onto the reef. To avoid catastrophe, support and supply ships sailed through a pass in the reef and entered the lagoon to unload in quiet water. The wrecked, damaged and non-running LVTs were in the way of these unloading activities as we tried to repair them.

Orders soon came to move our salvage and repair operations to a six- or so acre spot of bush-covered coral sand that lay on the east side of the reef, perhaps three miles south of Namur. This move put our company out of the way; it also put us out of sight of our division command.

We towed our shot-up and damaged LVTs down the lagoon to the tiny island. It took several days of steady work for us to create a wretched beach junk yard.

As our salvage operation was being completed, we saw our other three companies of LVTs and the division marines loading to leave. We were incredulous. No orders had come to us to prepare to load our LVTs and men into the LSTs (Landing Ships, Tank) which would carry us back to a base in the far distant Hawaiian Islands for rest, resupply and reorganization.

Our commanding officer set off in a frantic rush in one of our running LVTs to try to find out what was transpiring. Anxiety mounted in our men. Two things were clear: our ships were ready to sail away, and we were not aboard them. One by one the ships moved out of the lagoon by the deep northwest pass. The captain returned in despair. He had been given verbal orders for us to stay where we were.

We were in a terrible spot. We had no supplies of any kind and no designated way of getting any. The most immediate—and worst—problem was that we had no fresh water. This was an emergency; one cannot last long in the tropics without water. We had no food. We had no fuel for our LVTs. We had no medical supplies. We had no shoes. There was no clothing. There were no cooking utensils. We had no tents or other shelter. There was no source of spare parts or tools. We were desperate.

I have always believed that our awful situation was the result of an upper command, administrative oversight, followed by an effort to cover up the error.

My belief that we were placed in our predicament by mistake grew out of our captain's receiving verbal orders. We certainly should have had written orders for a major administrative move such as a detachment from our battalion. I never saw any written orders, and I suspect there weren't any—at least not at the time the verbal orders were given.

There is more, much more. Later, we found we were on no personnel roster.

We were on no pay schedule and got no pay. We received no mail for six months and had no contact with the outside world.

We had no mailing address.

Though we were supposed to receive them, we were given no unit citations for valor and superior combat operations.

Not only were we lost; we were gone!

Be all of the above as it may, we had an emergency. We had to get drinking water, and quickly. Our men begged some from ships lying to in the lagoon. We liberated some from a navy shore party which was bounteously supplied with everything. We later located and obtained, at night, a water distilling unit which we hid in the bushes and which probably saved the lives of some of our men who had diarrhea and severe dehydration.

Once we had our distilling machine, we could turn our efforts toward obtaining food. Begging parties were formed, some going to ships in the lagoon, others going to food supply dumps on Roi and Namur. I trained some of our men in locating and grabbing small octopi in crevices in the reef. We found a cache of small, black, Japanese hand grenades and two good-sized inflatable rubber boats drifting, unmanned, in the lagoon. We would float along, drop grenades and catch stunned fish by hand. We had a couple of breadfruit trees on our islet. Their fruits were soon eaten. Scouts found a dump of sealed, five-gallon tin cans of flour. They brought these back. Gradually, we collected enough to keep us going on a meal a day, plus anything we could pick up along the way.

Our cook did a valiant job. His only utensils were three galvanized garbage cans, a long-handled ladle made from a broomstick, and a wooden boat paddle for stirring. Two garbage cans were used for cooking. The third was used for lemonade. Our only source of vitamin C was a substance that came in fair-sized cans labeled "lemonade powder." It was some kind of awful ersatz mixture. Our cook would fill the galvanized garbage can with precious water, open a can of the powder, dump it in and stir it with the wooden boat paddle. The powder was so acid that the lemonade solution ate away the zinc galvanizing on the garbage can. Several men, including me, got scurvy.

It was the dry season. No rain fell for many days. There were no tents or other shelter. It took us a long time to scrounge scraps of canvas and several pieces of old, rusted, corrugated roofing tin. We made crude shelters. Gradually, we moved from moment-to-moment desperation to a more stable day-to-day misery.

I let you know all this so you can put into context some of the stories I am about to tell you. They start before we were a Lost Company and progress, more or less chronologically, until and after we were quietly and individually assigned to other units. After all, there is no way to disband a company that doesn't exist. A company lost and gone forever.

Curiosity

ALTHOUGH I AM not sure of the sequence, I believe that in our attack on Kwajalein, marines were landed on an island on the reef directly south of Namur just before the main landing on Roi and Namur. There was a large concrete building on the island with two steel radio towers, apparently a communications center. LVTs landed troops in the attack on this island.

Our LVT had been loaded with riflemen and a navy corpsman. There were only fighting men in the marine corps. Medical care was offered to our men by navy personnel. Corpsmen were attached to our marine units for first aid care. Many of these corpsmen were gutsy, brave people who were thought highly of by the men in the outfits to which they were attached. They were supposed to be unarmed, but our fighting was so intense and at such close quarter that most felt they had to be able to defend themselves. They appropriated the rifles of wounded marines they were called on to treat.

The battleships Maryland and Colorado had survived Pearl Harbor, been repaired and were detailed to the task force which attacked Kwajalein. They mounted two 16-inch guns in each of two turrets forward and two more 16-inchers in one turret aft. The ships' duty was to offer us fire support prior to and during our landings. They were stationed about 2000 yards—a bit over a mile—offshore from Roi and fired east toward Roi and Namur. This was point-blank range for them.

Those of you who have never seen a battleship fire a broadside have missed an awesome sight. About a quarter-acre of orange flame spouts from the mouth of each gun. Out of this flame emerges a 16-inch diameter, several foot long shell weighing over a ton and about one-third the size of a Volkswagen Beetle automobile. This massive round travels, at a guess, more than 2000 feet per second. The recoil is so great that I have seen a many thousand-ton ship shoved sideways in the water when firing a broadside. The streamlined shell goes through the air with an awful, ripping, tearing sound.

The Japs had an airfield on Roi that occupied much of the island. Alongside the field were two odd-looking structures. These were shaped a bit like giant, rounded loaves of French bread. They offered no flat surface for a shell or bomb to hit. Projectiles would tend to ricochet off them. They were built of a special, grayish concrete, so hard and tough that it was far, far beyond anything I have ever seen. The reinforcing steel within the concrete, instead of being the half-inch diameter, several-foot-long rods that I have seen used in our country, was full-length railroad rails welded together and imbedded deep in the concrete. The demonstrated strength of the material was beyond my comprehension.

Our battleships began to fire at these fortifications. I was astounded to see our immense shells ricocheting without even beginning to penetrate the concrete. Even though I saw it happening, I couldn't believe my eyes.

This went on while I was carrying an LVT full of riflemen and a corpsman across the lagoon to land on the communications building island. After a time our ships ceased firing, possibly in surprise at not being able even to crack the fortifications. The delay might have been that our ships were shifting to the use of armor-piercing projectiles. Though I have never seen a 16-inch armor-piercing shell cut open, I have seen smaller bore versions of such shells opened up. I suspect strongly that the 16-inch shells are much like the smaller ones. There is an outer layer of projectile which is made of tough steel. Inside this steel jacket is a large core of heavy, dense, exceedingly hard metal. When the projectile strikes, the outer steel jacket sticks to the target's surface for a thousandth of a second. The hard core is thereby supported and positioned to penetrate the resistant material of the target. The steel jackets usually strip off and can fly through the air for great distances. They are sharp and ragged-edged.

After our LVT and others like ours landed the riflemen on the communications island, I was called ashore on the island to see about something near its tip closest to Roi-Namur. As I got to where I was supposed to go, the Maryland and

the Colorado again started firing at the loaf-shaped fortifications. Ricochets were going in several directions, depending on how the shells struck the hardened, sloping concrete.
If you have ever had a .22 caliber bullet ricochet near you,
you know how unsettling it is, with its penetrating, zinging
sound. Now try to imagine how a ten thousand times larger
piece of ragged steel sounds as it passes you at a speed of
900 or so feet per second.

A ricochet passed me. I hit the deck and tried to hand-
scrape a hole in the sand, pitifully inadequate protection,
but all I could get. The scene was dramatic: the battleships
firing, the shells hitting the fortifications, an occasional ricochet coming toward us.

I peeked up to gauge how best I could get the hell out
of there. I saw the corpsman stand up to get a better look
at the wild scene. As he did, a several foot long piece of
ragged steel jacket, weighing perhaps two to three hundred
pounds, came shrieking through the air. It hit the corpsman
at just about his waist, not very neatly separating his upper
half from his lower.

Curiosity killed the corpsman.

The Explosion

IT WAS BEYOND belief. I was at least three-quarters of a mile away out in the lagoon at Kwajalein Atoll on the day of our attack on the islands of Roi and Namur. The shock wave at that distance was so great that I felt like I had been hit a double head and body blow with a baseball bat. It was as though the blow sank into the deepest parts of my body and did damage there. My head inside my steel helmet was dealt a blow so massive and deep that the amalgam fillings in my teeth were loosened and gave off metal. A strange taste filled my mouth.

After a few moments, pieces of material began to rain down into the water near our LVT and over a great distance beyond. We were hit only with small bits of concrete, no one was injured and our LVT was undamaged.

As I looked at the blast site, I saw a column of dark smoke starting near ground level and rising swiftly far up into the sky. Atop this rising column was a gigantic piece of concrete about three feet in thickness and perhaps a half-acre in width and length. Dangling railroad rails protruded from the concrete. This great mass of material sat atop the rising column of smoke almost like a bottle cap. As it rose higher into the sky, an 0S2U2 naval gunfire spotter plane pilot came on the radio and said in an awed voice, "That damn thing just passed me going up. I'm at 1400 feet."

For a second or two the mass seemed to stop rising and just hang in the air. It then started downward and dropped swiftly into a fresh crater where the blast had originated. While we stood transfixed, a large body part of a Jap soldier came toward us, tumbling over and over in perhaps a thousand-foot arc. I could see the wrapped cloth puttees still in place on both legs. Split-toe tennis shoes were on each foot. The Jap fell into the water some distance away.

My LVT crew and I had no idea what had happened. What I learned later was that the Japanese had a large, more or less rectangular, massive concrete building on Namur Island. It had three-foot thick, hardened concrete walls and roof with railroad rails embedded into the concrete as reinforcing rods. There was a large, thick steel door with hinges fixed deep into the concrete walls. As our marines approached the building in a fierce fire fight, a bunch of Japs jumped up and ran into it. They slammed and locked the heavy steel door behind them. There were no windows or openings of any kind in the walls of the building. They could not fire out and we could not get in.

Our marines called for a demolitions team. These people carried, amongst other explosives, a kind of munition called a "shaped charge." These were made of TNT shaped in a form roughly resembling a beehive. The base of the beehive was hollow and had adhesive around the rim. Our physicists had calculated the shape and form of the beehive so that when stuck to a wall, its hollow interior would direct the sun-hot gases and shock wave from the exploding TNT into a plume which would penetrate and break up the walls of fortifications.

Unbeknownst to our demolitions team, or any of the rest of our marines, was that the Japanese were using this building as a cache for torpedo warheads. Records recovered later indicated that they had 460 tons of warheads stored there. As the warheads detonated, the explosive force was contained and concentrated for a fraction of a second, somewhat like setting off a firecracker in a tin can. The great blast was magnified by the instant of containment within the walls of the building. Some of the energy was directed upward, and the building's roof was what the 0S2U2's pilot had seen going past him at 1400 feet.

We never knew whether our marines' shaped charges or the Japs in the building set off the warheads. Everyone in or near the building was killed.

Sometimes one can never know.

We have to leave it at that.

Lord, the Flies

PRIOR TO OUR assault on the small islands of Roi and Namur, a part of Kwajalein Atoll in the Marshall Islands, our intelligence estimated the Japanese defenders at about 4000 men. If each man weighed 150 pounds, probably a conservative figure, the total represented well over half a million pounds of Jap meat.

We killed almost every one of them, and almost all within two days of fighting. There was no way to bury them quickly, and they lay in the hot tropical sun for several days. The stench was appalling.

The Japs had not been any too neat to start with. They had a great many flies. Few, if any, natural enemies of flies were present. Houseflies and carrion flies have an immense capacity to reproduce and reproduce quickly in almost wholly favorable circumstances. Within a few days, the results of this monstrous reproduction were apparent. Flies were everywhere; their numbers were beyond counting; those numbers were even beyond the wildest imagining. I had never seen anything like this. I hope never to again.

Our landing ships and other supply vessels could not land or unload efficiently from the open sea side of the small islands of Roi and Namur. This meant that unloading had to be undertaken from the lagoon side of the islands, where there were coral sand beaches and quiet waters. We had many disabled LVTs, as well as almost nothing in the way of spare parts. Our Company's 30 to 40 LVTs took up considerable lagoon-side space as we tried to scavenge parts and get every LVT we could in running condition.

We were soon ordered to leave Roi and Namur, since we were in the way. We were further ordered to set up camp on a tiny, undisturbed island located about three miles down the reef from Roi and Namur. Our little islet had only a few acres above the high-water mark. It was covered with small bushes, had a couple of breadfruit trees, a number of large Pandanus bushes and a few stunted coconut palm trees. As we towed our disabled LVTs down the quiet waters of the lagoon, our temporary home-to-be looked like a paradise compared to the devastated Roi and Namur, where gunfire had almost wholly stripped the land of vegetation.

What we were not prepared for in our South Seas paradise islet were the flies. We were downwind of Roi and Namur. The flies, having bred in the dead Japs, emerged in monstrous numbers. They had no vegetation on Roi and Namur to rest on. They flew about there in immense swarms. These swarms often got caught up in the strong, steady wind and were blown over the sea toward our tiny islet. Once they got there, they landed. They landed in such numbers that strong, sturdy bushes were broken down by their weight. A twig the size of a broom straw might have flies resting on it and on each other on top of it, until it was stripped from the weight of the flies. One of these tiny twigs would have a mass of flies clinging to it that were the diameter of a man's wrist.

Soon after we landed and dragged our disabled LVTs onto the lagoon-side beach of our islet, I led several of our marines on a reconnaissance of our new home. As we moved up from the beach we came to the bush area. We had flies all over us, of course. They were in our eyes, noses, mouths. They clustered in great numbers on our sea-water-and-sweat-wet dungarees. We simply were not prepared for what we found in the bushes. The stronger twigs and the leaves which had not been stripped from their plants by the weight of the flies had great masses of flies resting upon them. As we moved cautiously through the bushes on our reconnaissance, we could not help shaking the vegetation through which we were trying to move. This disturbed the resting flies, which took wing in such inconceivable numbers that there was a great roar from the millions upon millions, perhaps even billions of concurrently beating wings. This roar was so loud and so penetrating that it felt like it was entering not only my ears but every part of my body.

In this awful mess, I observed something that may have been life-saving for us. The sky-darkening swarms of flies, when denied landing space on shaken bushes, tended to keep on flying and disturb other great masses of flies on nearby vegetation. These great swarms rose in the air until they were caught in the full force of the steady trade winds. Many—but sadly a long way from all—were blown out to sea and did not have the capacity to fly back and re-land.

As soon as our reconnaissance was complete and we found no Japs, we returned to our main body of troops, reported what we had found and ordered our men to walk shoulder to shoulder, shaking the branches of the bushes violently. We stirred up a gigantic swarm of flies, these were caught up in the wind and were sent on a long, one-way downwind journey out across the vast Pacific. We cheered them on their filthy way.

Though we repeated our maneuver many times and reduced our fly population by 90% or more, we still had many millions of flies left. These were a horror to us. They got in our eyes, our noses, our mouths and our rectums when we tried to have a stool.

We got terrible diarrhea from the bacteria carried by the filthy flies. We had no source of fresh water on the island. We knew how to drink the liquid from green coconuts by opening the stem end with great care but our potable liquid supply from the few nuts on our tiny island ran out within hours. We were reduced to begging water from ships in the lagoon. Our supply of water was sometimes so low that we rationed ourselves to two canteens per day for those of us who were well.

At any one time, about a third of our men had diarrhea. Perhaps a quarter to a third of these sick men had severe to massive diarrhea. Our situation was desperate. We had no authorized and dedicated source of water. Our men were rapidly becoming dehydrated, some so short of body fluids that they had a syndrome resembling cholera, with sunken eyes, skin pallor and a diminished level of consciousness. Knowing that we had men who were going to die, we adopted the only measures we had available. We stole water from a contingent of navy people who had been sent ashore on Roi-Namur with bounteous supplies of everything. We gave water to our sick men. This allowed us a few hours to invent something.

We located a trailer-mounted, gasoline-powered distilling unit that had not yet been put into use. We waited for night to fall after having towed two of our disabled LVTs into the water from our small beach. Their hulls were found to be intact and did not leak. We lashed them together and lashed boards onto their flat upper surfaces to make a crude platform. We got two operating LVTs and towed the lashed-together ones from our islet across the lagoon to a large crater in the reef which we knew about at the edge of the beach on Namur Island. With our operating LVTs in lowest low gear, we towed our two, lashed-together hulls across the reef and into the crater. They sank deep enough into the water in the crater so that the platform was only a few inches above the crater edge at the beach. With our hearts in our throats and our asses hanging out a mile had we been caught, we used the operating LVTs to ever so gently tow the trailer-mounted water-distilling unit onto our crude platform. We then switched tows and, again ever so gently, eased our disabled LVTs with their board platform and precariously-perched distilling unit across the reef and into the calm waters of the lagoon. Our trip back to our tiny islet was completed before dawn.

When we arrived at our reef and beach area, we reset our tows and pulled the disabled LVTs across the reef to a point where our beach went steeply into the foot or so of sea water on the reef. By pushing the sterns of the disabled LVT hulls, we were able to tip downward their pontoon-like, sloping bows onto the beach. We rolled the trailer with its mounted distilling unit from the rough board platform onto our beach. As dawn was breaking, we towed the trailer into the bushes, camouflaged it, pumped it full of sea water and started it. It operated without a hitch. In a couple of hours, we had fresh water to give our diarrhea-stricken and dehydrated men. We did not lose a single man to diarrhea and dehydration.

I hate filthy flies.

Adrift

OUR TWO INFLATABLE boats, those we had found in the lagoon, were towed ashore on our islet and examined carefully. One was in only fair condition, with chafed areas and some minor tears in its rubberized fabric. The other was in good, usable condition. We put it to use.

These boats were considerably less than ideal for our purposes. They were probably a bit more than ten feet long, black in color, and surprisingly heavy, making them clumsy and hard to maneuver. There was a rather poorly formed bow and something more or less resembling a stern. When used in the manner for which they were designed, they floated eight men with rifles and each with a paddle. For travel over short distances and with the eight men all paddling quietly, their speed was about two to three knots. Heavier paddling made little change in speed but would soon exhaust the packed-in men. Mostly the boats were used for quiet night landings, reconnaissance and special missions.

Our use was quite different. Two or three of us would set out to try to get fish to feed our men. Carrying a score or so of the small, cylindrical Jap grenades, we would float along in about ten to fifteen feet of water and parallel to the lagoon-side beach of our little islet. We had only a crude board and our hands for paddles and could only creep along over the surface at an agonizingly slow pace. We would look down into the water and try to spot schools of fish. When we saw such a school, we would strike the pin of a grenade and drop it in the water. Its several second fuse would allow the grenade to sink in the water before it detonated. The shock wave of the detonation would, if we were lucky, stun some of the fish and allow their swim bladders to let them rise a bit toward the surface of the sea.

None of us knew how to dive. We had, of course, no air tanks or breathing equipment and had to try to get down to the stunned fish by holding our breath and swimming down to them. One of our men had found, on a dead Jap, a pair of small, poorly-fitting, diving goggles which helped keep the stinging sea water out of the diver's eyes. At best, we could retrieve only a few of the grenade-stunned or killed fish.

Our attempt to feed our men and ourselves was risky, inefficient, and ecologically destructive. My only reply to these points is that we were desperate for food. Desperation makes justifiable extensive risks, considerable inefficiencies and much destructiveness. Unless you have, yourself, faced starvation in a literal sense, you have no foundation for criticism.

The entire attention of the three of us in the boat was directed toward not getting killed from a grenade exploding before it was deep in the water, spotting and recovering disabled or killed fish, and looking for new schools of fish to attack. For quite a long time we worked at our food gathering, so long a time that we looked up to find ourselves just past the lee of our island and drifting away from it under the influence of the steady trade wind. We frantically started trying to paddle back under the lee of the island and out of the wind, which was blowing us out into the many-mile -wide lagoon. We knew that there was only reef downwind of us, and no islands for many miles. It was near certain that after an hour or two of drifting we would be cast upon the reef only to be cut to death on the living coral. If, by chance, we drifted into one of the few passes in the reef, we would then be drifting without water into the vast Pacific.

I was the senior person in our three man crew. Mine was the responsibility for directing our activities and keeping us as free from harm as possible. I had failed in this and put us at great risk. The failure was mine and mine alone. I was about to get all three of us killed.

With our board paddle and with two of us hand paddling, we began frantically trying to regain a position in the lee. Were we able to do this, we could then gradually work ourselves back to shore. Everyone realized at once the terrible trouble we were in. We paddled until we dropped from exhaustion.

With no more than a hundred feet to go, we could have gotten out of the wind enough to save ourselves. We could see all this clearly. We were so utterly exhausted that we could not make that last one hundred feet. No one heard our calls for help. We were vomiting from extreme exertion. The wind again carried us toward the center of the lagoon.

I was terrified. We were going to get killed, and it was my lack of generalized attention to our position that had put us in this awful spot. My fatigue was so extreme from the hand paddling that I could only lie in my own vomit, too weak to move.

After a few minutes I recovered enough strength to look about and try to find a way to get us out of this awful predicament I had gotten us into. There didn't seem to be any. By then we were far out in the lagoon and getting farther every minute. We were drifting at an estimated four to four and a half knots, a great deal more than the one knot we could make by paddling. Our demise was near certain and only hours away. This sank into me with a cold terror.

One faint hope seemed to be that we could hand paddle south while we were being blown a bit south of west. Far down the lagoon, almost surely too far for us to paddle, was an uninhabited strand of sand with a few bushes and almost certainly no drinking water. If we could make it, which we had little chance of doing, we might be able to dig a hole in the coral sand near the center of the islet and get some brackish water to sustain us for a few hours or perhaps a day or two. From this sand spit we conceivably might be spotted by a reconnaissance aircraft. This was not much of a plan in terms of probable success, but it was enough to give us a sense of purpose and something to stave off our terror.

A Jap submarine, possibly damaged many days earlier by depth charges, had been run up onto the reef far down from our wee islet. Its crew had escaped, and the vessel had been abandoned. Several naval intelligence people had been sent down in a power boat to examine it. They had finished their work and were returning to Roi-Namur islands to report their findings.

By one chance in many millions, I looked up to see the powered landing craft with a half dozen or so men aboard. Though far away, it was on a course partially intersecting our drifting course. We waved frantically. After a time they saw us, changed course and came alongside. They threw us a line and towed us back to our island.

Sometimes, God, in His Grace, overlooks stupidity.

This time He did.

Diarrhea

I HAVE TOLD you about our many little friends, the filthy flies. They were the probable source of the life-threatening diarrheal illness we had soon after arriving at our South Seas paradise. Pristine initially, the island was, within days, awash in wet stool. The flies, of course, got into that. It was a mess.

The first wave of the squirts came on within a couple of days or so after our arrival, before we had any source of water other than what we could beg from ships anchored in the lagoon and waiting to unload. They soon got tired of our pleading and we were then down to what we could steal, which was little indeed.

Fresh water was so precious to us and our supply so perilously tentative that we were down to rationing two canteens a day to our well people and a bit more than that to our sick. In the first wave of illness, about one-third to one-half of our men were stricken at the same time. About a third of this half were seriously ill and in danger of extreme dehydration.

Our situation was obviously desperate; it called for desperate measures. We adopted these and obtained the distilling machine of which I have told you. Before we could

Figure 6. The Officers and NCO Mess

steal it, we had to wait for night to fall and then wait for the night-long slow towing down the lagoon to our island. This left us a near 24-hour period with large numbers of seriously ill men who were becoming, and rapidly becoming, more dehydrated. Our situation was critical.

We had no medical personnel. Not even a medical corpsman was on our roster. Navy doctors were attached to other marine organizations, but these people were responsible for treating the wounded. They had all they could possibly do, and more. A trip to ask for help from the hospital ship moored in the lagoon was met with, at first, disbelief and then derision. "What the hell are you doing here, Lieutenant, asking for a doctor to treat men with the shits. Get your ass off this ship." Asking again seemed less than worthwhile.

We were out of options. We had to do the best we could with the clear understanding that our comrades might die if our best turned out to be not enough. Our stimulus was intense. This intensity led to inventiveness.

After being so delicately rebuffed on our visit to the hospital ship and after climbing back into one of the few still running LVTs, we found ourselves near the shore of Roi Island at a place where supplies were being unloaded. We unobtrusively eased our LVT in between two LSTs and backed it in to the slanting beach so that the stern of the LVT would be high and our bow down near the water, thus partly hiding our cargo compartment. We dismounted and, one at a time, moved toward the working party people who were doing the unloading. This was dirty, hard, sweaty work for the people in the working party. They could not imagine anyone joining them who was not ordered to do so.

Our four or five people, me included, mingled with the men in the working party and began carrying boxes. These boxes, almost all of them, had a legend clearly marked on them naming their contents. When we came onto something in boxes with the writing indicating the contents might be drinkable liquid, we picked them up and started carrying them out of the ship and toward the pile of boxes on shore. We managed, time after time, to deviate from the line just as we came near our backed-in LVT. We loaded the boxes into our open but partly hidden LVT cargo compartment. We managed to secure perhaps a dozen, perhaps twenty boxes of four one-gallon cans of stewed whole tomatoes. Before we were discovered, we eased the LVT into the water and started our three-mile or so trip down the lagoon to our islet and sick men.

I knew nothing at that time about what is now well understood in medical practice in regard to replacement of fluids and salts in dehydrated patients. Through sheer good fortune, for which I am still grateful many, many years later, we had stumbled onto a fluid in the cans of stewed tomatoes which was mostly water, but which also contained appreciable amounts of the sodium, potassium, magnesium and chloride ions which our people had lost in their massive, watery diarrhea. Through further good fortune, for which I am also deeply grateful, the illness we had did not involve much nausea and vomiting. There was no means of our giving fluids intravenously, even if we had had them to give, which we, of course, did not. We were able to pour off the stewed tomato fluid and give it to our sick men to drink.

My friend, Lt. Gaebe, was amongst the most desperately ill. Though I am sure he did not have classical cholera, he did have a cholera-like syndrome with extreme dehydration, almost continuous diarrheal stools, sunken eyes, pallid skin, weak and rapid pulse, extreme weakness and diminished consciousness. Though I was not trained as a physician at that time, it was clear to me that he was near death.

I took one of the gallon cans of tomatoes and opened it with a bayonet. I had a canteen cup and poured fluid from the can into my canteen cup. I had no utensil of any kind and, while pouring, had to hold back the peeled but whole tomatoes with my fingers. Some of the tomato slipped through my dirty hand and fell into the canteen cup. There was no time to do anything delicate like fish for the lumps of tomato to pick them out of my canteen cup with a stick. If Gaebe were going to live, I had to get the fluid into him, and quickly.

I held up his head and let him drink from the cup. He was conscious enough to be able to drink and swallow. I gave him the contents of the cup a little at a time while beating off the flies. It took Gaebe perhaps fifteen minutes or more to take the fluid and pieces of tomato in the cup. He saved his life by not vomiting. After getting the fluid down, Gaebe did not look much better, but he stopped getting worse. This was progress. The progress led me to continue expressing fluid from the tomatoes by squeezing them in my hand and draining the fluid into my canteen cup. Bits of tomato fell into the cup. Gaebe was able to hold this down as well. He never vomited a single time.

His diarrhea slowed. Some time passed between Gaebe's first ingestion of the fluid with its bits of tomato and his having a large, almost clear, watery stool. Contained in the stool was a soft bit of reddish material about the length of, but not the thickness of, the outer joint of one's little finger. I feared when I saw it that it was a piece of blood-tinged intestinal mucosa (intestinal lining tissue) that had sloughed off and been expelled. If, indeed, the small mass was a bit of bloody mucosa, it was a dire sign. With intense concern, I looked carefully at the soft red mass in the nearly clear, watery stool. I gave a sigh of great relief when I saw a number of small seeds fixed in the mass. It was a bit of the mashed tomato that I had given him less than an hour before. Though I have never looked it up in the literature, this may be near a record for portal-to-portal, lips to anus, passage of material entirely through the many feet of an adult human's gastro-intestinal tract.

Record-holder or not, Gaebe got better.

Moray Eels

I HAD ALWAYS heard of moray eels as being formidable creatures, certainly not to be messed with. This was particularly the case after my reading an article which described the amazing power of their snapping jaws and the severing capacity of their sharp and rugged teeth. Included in the article was a picture of a human, his right forearm terribly injured, with a triangular, pie shaped segment missing. The moray had bitten through both sides of one of his forearm bones (the radius) so that the bitten off piece of bone lay in its original position within the severed piece of arm tissue. The jaws were so strong and the eel's teeth so sharp that the arm and the cut out piece looked like they had been surgically separated.

Before I ever got to the Marshall Islands, I was quite clear that being around moray eels was not in my best interests. This proved to be true in two situations of sudden surprise while I was in the Marshalls.

I have told you earlier of our desperate search for food in the early days of the Lost Company's being orphaned. Part of that struggle was trying to catch young octopi from crevices and pockets in the coral reef on which our islet sat. Our men and I would cruise the reef at low tide looking for octopi small enough to catch by hand without getting hurt. Bigger ones could give the captor a nasty cut by wrapping their arms around his arm and dragging their hard beak across the captor's flesh. These cuts did not heal well, offering yet another reason to be careful. Still, we persisted. They were food and we were hungry.

The magnitude of the tides on the reef at Kwajalein, in the middle of the Pacific, were greater than I had expected. I had read that tides in an ocean far from a large land mass were slight in their range from high to low. The appearance of a considerable difference in tide heights may well have been added to by the minimal elevation of our tiny islet above high water level. Whatever the reasons, our section of lagoon-side reef at lowest tide levels was at sea level or barely above it for about an hour on some days.

At one of these times, I was searching the reef. I came upon a piece of partly-rounded coral rock about the size of five or six basketballs. It weighed perhaps one-hundred-twenty-five to one-hundred-eighty pounds and appeared to have been broken off the sea-side reef by the pounding waves. This pounding was so heavy at times that when I lay on the ground at night to sleep, I could feel the island trembling beneath me.

Hoping to find an eating-size octopus beneath the rock, I rolled it over. There was no octopus, but out from under the boulder came two wet creatures that looked like hyperactive snakes. They were each no more than fourteen to sixteen inches long, perhaps five times the diameter of a lead pencil and mean as hell. I had really pissed them off. They were going to make me pay for disturbing them, and right away too. They raised the forward three to four inches of their bodies and began snapping their jaws as they crawled toward me. These little things had jaws so powerful that their snapping sound was like that of a steel trap springing shut. It was clearly audible and just as clearly vicious and menacing. I had to move quickly and then run away to keep from getting nastily and repeatedly bitten. They were young moray eels.

My second experience with moray eels was absolutely terrifying. Many weeks later than my first experience, we were at Namorick Atoll, a remote spot some considerable distance from Kwajalein.

We had landed our marines on the sea side of the small, two-island atoll. We were fortunate not to have any Jap fire on the beach and equally fortunate to have wave and reef conditions that allowed a sea-side landing without loss of a single LVT. These conditions, however, were certainly a lot less than ideal for us. They might worsen at any time. We had to land more men and supplies.

It was quite apparent that we needed a better landing area if we could find one. I went with my crew in our LVT through a shallow pass in the reef and into the lagoon to search for a lagoon-side place where wave, reef and water conditions would be more favorable and more predictable.

Such a landing spot might, however, be impractical for two major reasons. First, it might be mined. The Japanese had two types of quite dangerous beach mines. They would plant them in about twenty-inch deep water and parallel to the line of the beach. They were known to us as one-tit and three-tit mines. The one-tits were conical in shape, rather like an inverted metal funnel. The spout of the funnel faced toward the surface of the sea and closely resembled a cow's teat, except for several ringlike ridges and a lead color. The teats were rounded and closed at the top but thin-walled and hollow. The interior was filled with, as best we could determine, a liquid acid. When broken by an LVT track, boat hull or other means, the acid was released. An electrical current supposedly was generated. This set off a detonator which in turn detonated the eleven pounds of picric acid explosive contained within the steel, funnel-shaped base. The base was planted firmly in the beach sand. When the mine was detonated by crushing of the soft metal teat, its explosive force was directed upward. The cursed things would blow off an LVT track in an instant. Depending on several factors, the LVT hull might or might not be breached at the same time. They were hard-to-spot, nasty little bastards.

Far, far nastier were the three-tits. They had the same kind of nipples, but these were fixed to a thirty-three pound, picric acid explosive charge. The yellow, solid picric acid was contained in something rather similar in shape to a cow's udder.

The udder was made of steel and painted a dull, blu-ish-gray. Its three teats were arranged around the curved, or domed, top while the bottom was flat—a three-teat steel udder that would blow you to hell in an instant. These, too, were hard to see. I feared them.

The second major reason a lagoon-side landing site might be impractical was the possible presence of large cor-al heads. These might protrude upward and impale our thin steel LVT hulls.

Either of these two possibilities would make the hoped-for landing site too dangerous to use except in an ex-treme emergency.

It was up to me to look over the potential landing area before orders were given to use it. With many of our men's lives depending on the accuracy of my observations and judgment, I had to use great care in looking over the under-water part of the proposed crawl-out spot.

My two great concerns were those I have described above: just-underwater beach mines and deeper-water cor-al heads. It was best to start with the coral heads. If there were none, we could slowly and gently work our clumsy hull into position where I could stick my head under water and open my eyes for the few moments that I could toler-ate the seawater sting, and look for beach mines ahead of us while we were still afloat in shallow water.

This may all sound simple and easy. It wasn't. Our crew was skilled, our driver expert. They were going to do their job of maneuvering the LVT. It was up to me to do my job of observing and estimating.

To this end, I ordered our driver to hold the steering brake on the starboard side track while letting the port track run free at about one-third engine speed. This would cause our hull to rotate clockwise, forming a "slick" on the surface so that I could see all the way to the bottom. I had positioned us so that the sun was above and behind us.

As the slick began to form, I placed my back to the sun, my face and head within a few inches of the surface and looked down into the crystal clear water. The closer I put my face to the water, the better I could see. My nose was almost in the water when my view of the irregular coral bottom was suddenly blocked. My blood froze as I realized I was looking directly into the open jaws of a gigantic moray eel. The eel's head was the diameter of a large dinner plate. Its great long body came partly out of a dark hole in the coral at least seven or eight feet below the surface of the sea. Its head was no more than a foot from my face. Had it snapped, its jaws could easily have severed my head and neck from my shoulders in one bite. I have no idea of what happened next. I was frozen with terror and amnesic for a time.

My next remembered thoughts were bizarre. I wanted to go across the lagoon to the small island forming the other part of the two-island atoll. There were four lepers living there. My fear of acquiring leprosy, though great, was infinitely less than the eel terror, from which I continued to tremble. I later had nightmares of that great gaping mouth and those awful, evil, staring eyes.

How would you like to have the inscription on your tombstone read, "Eaten by an eel"?

Figure 7. Men of the Lost Company.

Failed Command

YOUNG MEN IN our company, green to combat in the fighting at Kwajalein Atoll, had a fascination with fired, but unexploded, ordnance. Any slightest disturbance of a bomb could set if off. Its fuse has already been armed and could be activated by alteration of the position of the shell, by vibration, pressure, heating or other stimuli.

Such unexploded shells are termed "duds." In our training, we had had countless admonitions never to touch, move, disturb or even come near a dud. Despite all this, our people had some awful, deadly need to fool with duds—to pick them up, touch them or even to look at them from a few inches away.

I've wondered about this need, so suicidal in the face of the known danger. It goes far beyond mere curiosity, though curiosity certainly is a component, especially in men with no prior experience in combat. A major part of this awful need to fool with something that may well kill one and one's friends may come from feelings about one's own mortality, certainly at the forefront of one's being in active fighting. You think: "That shell lying there might have been the one that got me, but didn't. I had better examine it carefully to see what it is really like. Maybe it will help me dodge the next one. Also, it is an enemy, and I had better make sure the damn thing is really dead."

In a darkly humorous manner, this is a paradox. In an attempt to ensure one's survival, one engages in activity which will probably result in one's death. Perhaps one might better reply with another paradox: "I will take the risk of not finding out more about the shell that could have killed me by leaving it alone, thereby increasing my chances for survival. Oh well, what the hell."

Be all of that as it may be, we had only been on our tiny islet at Kwajalein for a couple of days when I saw one of our men pick up and look at a dud shell which had been partly buried in the coral sand. It was about 35 to 40mm in diameter, probably a 37mm that one of our own turret-mounted LVTs had fired with its small cannon. If it was one of our 37mm shells, it was exceedingly dangerous.

I told our man to take it at once, and carefully, out into the deep water of the lagoon and let it sink. I told him not to toss it but just to let it sink from his hand into the water. We had earlier found two rubber boats floating in the lagoon, and he could go out to deep water in one of these.

I turned away from him and walked over to talk with my friend, Lt. Gaebe, about how to undertake some repairs on our damaged LVTs. We needed to get as many as we could in running condition as quickly as possible.

This was a matter of great and immediate importance.

We were isolated without running LVTs. Gaebe and I sat down on five-gallon cans of flour to try to plan our efforts. We had a five-gallon can between us.

There was the sharp crack of an explosion. A piece of brass 37mm fuse passed between Gaebe and me, lodging deep in the flour can that sat between us. The man who had had the dud was lying on the ground with his left foot attached to a portion of his left lower leg only by his Achilles tendon. He had multiple wounds over the rest of his body. He died. Fourteen other men had wounds. The right side of my face and head was numb. The eardrum of my right ear was blown in. I was deafened. My problems were minor compared with those of the others. One of our people had a large, tearing, ragged shrapnel wound in his abdomen with perforation of the bladder. He later died.

The man who detonated the shell was seen by several of our people to be tapping the shell against a palm log in an attempt to straighten its bent tip. This was stupid beyond belief. I have wondered for years about this man's unconscious suicidalism and homicidalism. There was no question that he had disobeyed a direct, specific and immediate order.

I have wondered for years, as well, about my own lack of capability in command. My inability to have my order carried out resulted in the deaths of two men and the wounding of thirteen others.

I have had to live with that.

Dentistry

THE MEN OF our Lost Company reacted to the stress of our severe to desperate privations, combined with constant demands for more and more combat operations, in several different ways. Some quietly slept whenever they could manage any free time. Others sat and stared out at the empty sea. Others beat on a palm log with a stick to make noise.

Private First Class Kauskas was quite different. He spent much of his time looking for Jap corpses, of which there were initially a bounteous supply. The rest of his time he spent in fashioning a wee scabbard for a pair of pliers he had won from a swabbie in a poker game. He made the scabbard with considerable creativity from a torn-up leather pistol holster he got from a marine heavily hit by mortar shrapnel. He managed to form the scabbard so that it fit on the web belt of his dungaree trousers. In turn, it held snugly his precious pliers, a highly-valued tool in our desperately-deficient circumstances.

For a time none of us saw any connection between his two major activities. Part of this lack of association came out of Kauskas himself. He stank. He didn't stink delicately, he stank in an assertive, gagging, foully offensive manner. As best anyone knew, he had always stunk. On the other hand, he had grown up in the Great Depression and was all his life used to deprivation. Our desperate circumstances with limited drinking water, a terrible plague of carrion and houseflies, no reliable food source, no spare clothing, no bedding, and no shelter were an irritant but not that much out of the ordinary in his experience of life. Further, he was tough and resilient. He would, could and did fight like hell. These latter characteristics far offset his major drawback. After all, the rest of us with no change of clothing, no fresh water to bathe in and living in high humidity were ripe ourselves, just less consistently so. Kauskas was accepted and valued as one of us in the Lost Company.

His interest in Jap corpses caused him to stink even worse, particularly when he was seen to be straddling them and reaching into their mouths with his pliers, which he kept with him at all times. This was long before our current-day, generalized depravities, and no one even suspected him of necrophilia. Still, his frequent messing with corpses and his awful body odor called attention to him.

He was fascinated with the Japs' bright metal bridge-work. Some of these were probably of gold or silver, but their ultimate monetary value was not his interest. Rather, his interest was aesthetic. Somehow, somewhere, Kauskas had gotten hold of a fair-sized piece of white butcher paper. He kept this paper neatly folded in a waterproof oilskin sack along with his teeth. He would carefully unfold and lay out his paper in a sunlit spot and arrange the shiny gold-and-silver-colored teeth on it in contrasting patterns. This aesthetic activity caused us no problem; we were so totally taken up with trying to survive from day to day that a minor distraction was of no consequence.

After a time, though, things began to get out of hand. Kauskas had salvaged a sandbag from a revetment, poured out the sand, washed the bag in seawater to get out the rest of the sand and was using it as a pillow. It smelled terrible and finally caught his platoon sergeant's eye.

Alas, our man had slipped over from aesthetics into osteology. Teeth had finally gotten to him. He was no longer pulling bright, shiny metallic caps and bridgework. Now he was after just teeth, canines and molars preferred. He had an entire sandbag, the one he was using as a pillow, full of regular teeth. These were lovingly and carefully extracted; not a one was carious, broken or damaged. He really, really liked teeth.

Kauskas had finally crossed the line. We could have called in League of Nations officials, navy psychiatrists, social workers and other such second-level corrective persons to testify in mitigation as to Kauskas' deprived childhood. In our miserable circumstances, it seemed imperative to use direct, first-level measures instead.

We did this. Our gunnery sergeant was a formidable man. He had been, prior to World War II, the 185-pound boxing champion of the U.S. Asiatic Fleet. He had a broken,

twisted nose. There was scar tissue over much of his face
and head. He brooked no foolishness. If you had to pick one
of ten thousand men to mess with, the last one would be the
gunny.

We ordered Gunny to take care of the situation. He did
this in his own direct way. He walked over to Kauskas,
picked up his pillow sandbag of teeth, emptied the teeth
out and threw them into the sea along with the sandbag.
He grabbed Kauskas by the throat and lifted him onto his
tiptoes so that Kauskas had to stand at his ultimate height
to keep breathing. Gunny pulled Kauskas' face to within
about five inches of his own scarred face and flattened nose.
In a quiet, almost toneless voice he said, "Look, you filthy,
stinking, son-of-a-bitch, you mess with a dead Jap again, I
will beat you to a bloody pulp, throw your rotten ass down
on the ground and piss in your mouth while you strangle."
This was not a threat; it was an irrevocable life sentence.

Gunny's gentle admonition attracted Kauskas' attention. He never went near a Jap corpse again.

So ended an active and promising professional career.

Dugout Doug

I WAS ASTOUNDED when I got back to the States after a long time overseas to find that Douglas MacArthur was a great war hero and being touted for president in the upcoming national elections. We saw him overseas as a wonderfully successful publicity hound but military incompetent.

Never having met the man myself, my beliefs were founded on what I saw and heard, some of which was first hand, some not.

In the first place, General MacArthur was caught flat-footed when the Japs attacked the Philippines. Our B-17 bombers were under his direct command in what was then known as the Army Air Corps. They were caught sitting unmanned on the ground. I heard they were all destroyed.

After some fighting and repeated defeats, our troops in the Philippines, including marines, were withdrawn to the island fortress of Corregidor, trapped with no way out. The Japs attacked. Good old Mac set himself up in just about the only safe place, a tunnel dug deep in the island's rock. This, early on, is where he earned his almost universally used overseas nickname of Dugout Doug.

After receiving orders from above, he turned over command to his subordinate, General Wainwright, and left his trapped men. I have been told that he slipped out in the middle of the night on a high speed PT boat with his grand piano strapped to the plywood foredeck of the tiny vessel.

Mac set up shop in Australia, far from the fighting by the Australians in Papua, New Guinea, and by our marines in the Solomon Islands. I have been to the site of that headquarters. The location is on the high rim of a long inactive volcano, its crater filled with deep, cool, clear, fresh water. One looks out above the crater to see the great, wide, twenty-two-hundred-foot elevation valley known as the Atherton Tablelands. This valley is protected by the Gilles Range of mountains to the east and the Great Dividing Range to the west. It is a beautiful, quiet, safe, cool place with rampant blossoming bougainvillae and hibiscus.

In this war-torn, terrible setting, Dugout Doug set up an elaborate headquarters. His headquarters had a large—really large—group of what were called "puppy dog" war correspondents, many of whom never got closer to the fighting than paraphrasing the bulletins put out by Doug's own staff. The correspondents were so much under the great man's will that some of them lived up to the puppy dog sobriquet. When he noticed one of them and individually spoke to him, the man was so ecstatic that, figuratively, he might roll over on his back, wiggle around and wet himself. He would then write an article about the heroism of the great man. Perhaps this was the start of Doug's stateside reputation.

Part of the information we had on our mission when we were sent to the Solomon Islands from our islet at Kwajalein Atoll was that MacArthur was planning to "invade" an undefended island on his "I shall return" route back to the Philippines. We were told that he needed his left flank protected. Protected from what was never clear. We were to protect that supposedly threatened flank by an attack on far away Kavieng, where the Japs reportedly had no ships but forty thousand men and a number of tanks. Thank goodness, someone somewhere in some authority stopped what was deadly military idiocy.

Perhaps on this undefended island, but probably on another similar one, Doug and his publicity corps set up what has since come to be known as a "photo op." Though there was no fighting, MacArthur was scripted to step ashore from a landing craft in his best fighting-man stance, with crushed, "salty dog" frame cap, far-into-the-distance command stare, and corncob pipe. The problem with the script was that part of his heroism was to be recorded for posterity by a great group of already onshore photographers; these people needed a dead Jap to be thrown in the water as Doug stepped over the body to wade ashore. The essence of the script problem was that, since the island was undefended, there was no dead body available to throw in the water for Doug to step over as the flash bulbs popped and the cameras whirred. To resolve this emergency, a dead Jap from one of our marine operations was placed on a C-47 aircraft with no other cargo. First things first. The body was delivered and thrown in the water as the landing vessel's ramp dropped and Doug stepped out to wade ashore. One of the crewmen of the C-47 aircraft told me about this heroic MacArthur episode. I saw the pictures later and consider it quite probable the story is true.

After Doug finally fought his way back to the Philippines, there was another photo op, one of a great host of others. This op was similar in some respects to the one above in that Mac was to wade ashore on one of the Philippine Islands and announce "I have returned" to the accompaniment of flashing lights and clicking camera shutters. This script went well indeed until a flunky brought Doug a towel, dry socks and a new pair of shined oxford shoes. In the interval while this proceeded the photographers looked around for other things to record on film. They saw and began to photograph a marine howitzer battery, its cannons now secured and cleaned up after the fighting had ended. On the barrel of one of these hung a neatly lettered sign. It read "With the help of God and a few marines, MacArthur returns to the Philippines." Pictures were actually being taken of this blasphemy and snickering could be heard.

Doug went absolutely ballistic. Film was said to have been destroyed. Court-martials were threatened. I do not know whether any of the pictures survived, but the story was widely circulated.

Mac did a good job in Japan after the fighting ended.

He managed to replace Emperor Hirohito in the Japs' minds as a semi-deity and head of state. He may have been the only person whose ego was greater than that of the Japs' God-Emperor. After all, you've got to use the resources you have.

Much later Doug made a mess in Korea. He, again, got caught flatfooted when the Chinese came swarming across their border as our troops approached it. Mac withdrew, leaving the marines to try to fight off the hordes of Chinese in bitter cold. In one company of marines, only thirty-four survived. A lot of good marines are dead, courtesy of Dug-out Doug.

As I said earlier, much of the above comes out of things I have been told, sometimes second or third hand. The following is an otherwise unpublicized incident involving Doug, which was told to me first hand by one of the participants.

Our national position in the Korean War was carefully and skillfully set up by U.S. State Department people, with the association of a number of nations, among these Holland. The Dutch sent some of their marines to fight alongside our people. As you can imagine, the situation was delicate, delicate indeed, and required the greatest respect by everyone toward our allies.

The Dutch marines, a crack outfit, were manning a particularly dangerous section of our defense and being probed constantly by the North Koreans. Their attacks could be expected at any moment. Into this parlous and tense situation, in darkness, came the Supreme Commander, Dugout Doug. A marine sublieutenant was the field commander. His ancestors had served the Dutch monarchy continuously in their marine corps since the sixteenth century. This young officer was beautifully trained, a born commander, stubborn as only Dutchmen and Scotsmen can be. In addition, he was a giant of a man whose chest must have been two and a half feet thick from front to back—what is sometimes known, respectfully, as a great big f------g Dutchman.

This man greeted Doug and his entourage with due military courtesy but with the full knowledge that all the consequent hubbub might precipitate a North Korean attack. The supreme commander's first action was to light his corncob pipe. This was arrogant far beyond simple stupidity. It literally invited an artillery shell with more to follow. Arrogant, arrogant, and supremely stupid.

The sublieutenant instantly said, with great intensity and in excellent English "Sir, the smoking lamp is out." This means to put out any spark and not light another. The supreme commander, Old Dugout Doug, drew himself up to his full height, by the way less than that of the immense sublieutenant, and said, "Son, do you know who I am?"

Without a moment's hesitation the sublieutenant's reply came. "Yes, sir, I do, sir. The smoking lamp is still out".

Again, Doug went ballistic. He threatened the sublieutenant with court-martial. Doug perhaps had never met a really stubborn, tough Dutchman before. Doug's threats got him nowhere with this officer's refusal to have his men's lives threatened by such appalling, idiotic arrogance.

In the face of the delicacy of the situation with our ally, Doug followed through with his threat. As supreme commander, he ordered the Dutch commander to court-martial the sublieutenant. To the Dutch commander's credit, he did not buck it up the line and make an international incident of the inconceivably senseless matter. He court-martialed the sublieutenant, stripping him of his rank. The next day he quietly promoted the man two ranks. Doug never knew about this, apparently. The whole thing went no further.

Still later, MacArthur came back to the States as a great publicity-fabricated hero. He spoke to both houses of Congress at the time President Truman fired him. This was the occasion of his "Old Soldiers Never Die, They Just Fade Away" speech. Congressmen and senators were literally sobbing in the aisles.

The man was a dramatist, not a warrior.

Light in the Night Sky

WE WERE EMBARKED aboard a personnel transport vessel on a voyage from our islet at Kwajalein Atoll to the Solomon Islands. She was a deluxe ship compared to the LSTs (Landing Ship, Tank) that were our usual transport. We had a full ration of good food, all the water we wished to drink, and fan-ventilated below-decks areas to bunk in.

Our ship was of German design and fabrication. The Krauts had done a good job with her. Though a long way from new, she was tight as a drum with no twisting deformity of her hull in a heavy sea. She had a steady, 17-second roll. Her propulsion was smooth and even, with propellers which cut through the water smoothly without appreciable vibration. Her open upper deck was mostly free of hatches and cargo-working gear. I could lie on a smooth, steel deck at night and look at the exquisite southern hemisphere tropical sky with its velvety darkness and brilliant stars, seen without air pollution and distortion of their light.

Our ship had been caught in a Canadian or U.S. port at the beginning of WW II. She was possessed by our people and renamed the William P. Biddle. Her nickname was "The Lucky Willie P." She had been in a line of five ships which were attacked. Four of the five were hit. She survived without a scratch and went on much later to carry us at around fourteen knots for three weeks on a voyage whose route has always been a puzzle to me. From the Marshalls to the Solomons is, at a guess, about two thousand miles. We travelled at fourteen knots for twenty-four hours a day for twenty-one or twenty-two days. If my arithmetic is correct, that is about seven thousand miles. I never knew why we took the circuitous route we did and was in no position to ask questions to find out why. My guess then and my guess now is the same. Our route was taken because of threat of Japanese naval attack. This guess was reinforced by our having a cruiser and several destroyers as escort. The cruiser—perhaps she was the Santa Fe—repeatedly launched her 0S2 U2 pontoon-equipped reconnaissance aircraft, even in periods of heavy seas, when recovery of the aircraft was dicey indeed. In one of these recovery attempts while she was off our port bow, a man was lost overside from the cruiser. She continued her course without an attempt to recover him. Instead, a destroyer on our starboard quarter apparently was ordered to attempt a recovery. These were emergency maneuvers carried out in grim circumstances apparently arising out of a threat of attack.

The destroyer may have been the Anderson. Possibly her number was #411 or possibly #396. I tended to confuse her with a sister vessel, the Blue. Both destroyers were sometimes called N. R. A. ships because they were, I was told, built in the late years of the Depression under some kind of financing through the National Recovery Administration. Our national policy then was to try to stimulate our economy by using expensive materials. These small ships were fabricated with the finest metals. I heard their decks were stainless steel. They had a single trunked stack which exhausted combustion gasses from what must have been forward and aft inline-mounted boilers. These ships, their sailors claimed, were only about four thousand tons displacement—a small fraction of the displacement of current day destroyers. They had enormous power for their size and could do—this may well be their sailors bragging—close to forty knots at flank speed.

When the Anderson got the word of a man overboard from the cruiser, she lit off everything she had, including the chief's coffee pot. A great blast of soot, caked carbon and smoke erupted from the trunked stack. Her propellers began to turn so fast that they forced water from under her stern in such great volume that the entire stern sank below sea level. Her stern actually went down several feet. She shot forward, parallel to us, suddenly making well more than twice our speed. Her helmsman suddenly set her into a flank turn to port while she was still accelerating. This put her dead across our bow. She cleared us, moving like a steel spear through the water, by no more than a couple of hundred feet. Sadly, despite these efforts, the man in the water was never found.

I tell you all this so that you may have some sense of

the joy we had, with plenty of food and water, dry sleeping quarters, and rest, mixed with what obviously was concern in our flotilla's commander of a Japanese naval attack. Shipboard life settled in like this for many days until we began to near our destination in the Solomon Islands.

One quiet, clear, relatively cool night I was lying on the open deck, resting and enjoying the starlit sky. From time to time, I would arise and move toward the bow of our ship to watch the glowing, greenish, bioluminescence in the agitated sea water as our bow waves lapped over. Flying fish leaped from the water with a flash of light, moved through the air for a considerable distance, then re-entered the water with another cool, greenish flash. This was the beauty and enchanted restfulness of night at sea in quiet waters of the South Pacific, underlain, as always, by tension about our being attacked.

It was in this mixed context that I noticed a faint and varying, faraway diffuse light several degrees above the horizon and clearly well above anything floating on the sea. One possibility that concerned me almost instantly was that this was naval gunfire. Another was that it was a thunderstorm. The more I watched, the less the flashes resembled gunfire. They were slower, of an odd reddish to yellowish flare at times and had a persisting glow from what may have been the undersurfaces of clouds. Our night was perfectly clear, and an isolated thunderstorm out over the open sea was improbable. I suspected that we, on our circuitous route, were south of our destination at Guadalcanal in the Solomon Islands. As best I can recall there was a chain of islands nearby (the Santa Cruz?). The light was in the sky off our port bow, a position consistent with where I thought the islands might lie. Thunderstorms do form at times over islands in the middle of the night hours.

The longer I watched, fascinated and still concerned, the nearer our ship came to what looked like a fixed position of the origin of the light. I watched for hours—indeed, most of the night.

The light grew brighter as we came closer. I now could see a large mass of moving cloud over a mountain. There was a reddish glow reflected from the bottom of the cloud. The glow varied in intensity. There were, from time to time, and at irregular intervals, periods of much brighter reddish-orange light.

I was baffled, never having seen anything like this, certainly nothing like it in the dramatic and magical circumstances in which I found myself. Mysterious things are life-giving. I was fascinated, invigorated, and filled with vitality. Suddenly, with no prompting of any kind, I realized what I was seeing. Indeed, there was an island off our port side. Glowing dust clouds rose above a mountain. That mountain was a volcano. It was erupting.

If one allows it, beauty can reveal itself suddenly and unexpectedly in the most threatening of circumstances.

I now share that beauty with you.

Whitetit and Charlie

WE WERE ON an awful voyage from Tulagi in the Solomons to the assault on Saipan, and later Guam, in the Marianas. Look on your map now. It's a hell of a ways at 12 knots on an LST with 400 souls. Most of the men were from the Raiders, amongst the best, most disciplined and courageous troops in the Marine Corps. They were "old hands" with earlier fighting in many of the grim and loss-filled early operations in the greatest naval war in history. Truly, the crème de la crème.

Amongst these men, bound together by intense personal bonds forged in combat, were Whitetit and Charlie. Whitetit, known by no other name, had been massively burned by flamethrower liquid over his right chest, abdomen and right upper arm. Scar tissue and depigmented, dead-white skin had grown where it had been grafted over his upper body area in a wrinkled sheet. This contrasted starkly with the sunburned skin of the rest of his torso. Somehow, his scarred, twisted, and enlarged nipple had survived the burn and caught one's attention like the period of an exclamation point.

When shirtless, as we all were in the stifling tropical

heat on the deck of the crowded ship, Whitetit stood out.

Charlie, known by no other name, was a man who blended into the background. He was neither tall nor short, average in every aspect except for the expression around his eyes. Though not overtly threatening, it was so steely that even the least cautious fellow marine knew instinctively not to mess with him. I never heard him even raise his voice; he didn't have to. People left him alone

Whitetit and Charlie were inseparable, brothers-in-arms, members of a flame-thrower team. Charlie was there when Whitetit's nozzle was hit by an enemy round and when the fluid was burning his chest. Whitetit's gasping for breath in the agony of his burning had drawn flame into his lungs, resulting in pulmonary edema. He nearly died from lack of oxygen exchange in his fluid-filled lungs.

Charlie breathed for him for the first worst minutes by lifting his chest, taking some of the burned flesh with him as he tried to save his friend. After he got Whitetit stabilized a bit to where he could breathe precariously on his own, he proceeded to drag him along the ground under heavy enemy small arms fire.

Whitetit was so badly burned that there was little place on his upper right body to hold onto so as to drag him. The flesh would come off in Charlie's hands. Charlie stripped off his own dungaree jacket, spread it on the ground and placed Whitetit onto it by tugging on his helmet and lifting his entire upper body onto the jacket. Charlie then slid

Whitetit along the rainforest floor a few inches at a time. As he lifted, Charlie had to expose both of them to the intense enemy fire. He got a round through his left arm at this time. He staunched his own blood flow, then went back to inching Whitetit along toward a tiny rise in the ground which would offer them protection from the continuing rifle and automatic weapons fire. Charlie then crawled back to where he could find a medical corpsman. They got a stretcher, crawled back to Whitetit, rolled him onto it and inched him back to where they had a bit of cover and could stand up enough to carry the litter, with Whitetit on board, to the battalion aid station. Whitetit and Charlie both survived. They returned to duty to go with us on the awful 68-day voyage to the Marianas.

As we loaded the LVTs for the passage into the beach for the first waves of assault at Agat, I saw Whitetit and Charlie, together and with their flame-thrower, getting into their LVT.

I never saw them again.

A Gentleman, Later Commandant

AFTER LANDING THE first and then two following waves of marines on Agat beach in the assault on Guam, we were returning to our support ships to load and carry in mortar shells and flame-thrower materials.

We saw directly ahead of our LVT a destroyer escort. These beautiful little vessels were about one-third to one-half the size of a Fletcher-class destroyer and were used for all sorts of missions. The one ahead of us was standing in perilously close to the reef. We could not understand what she was doing in this position. It soon developed that she was the command support vessel for the First Provisional Marine Brigade, our landing force.

A major, standing near the destroyer's stern with another man, was motioning to us in an imperious manner to come alongside. Though he almost surely didn't know it, coming alongside a vessel at sea in an LVT was considerably more dangerous than it might seem to the uninitiated.

Our LVT hulls, to save weight, were fabricated of exceptionally thin metal. This metal was so thin as to be difficult to weld. The welds would sometimes split long-ways with a heavy lateral blow. The LVT would sink like a rock in a few seconds, often trapping the driver, who had to exit through a narrow, rear-facing hatch. To avoid this kind of catastrophe, the LVT driver had to come alongside the larger vessel at an acute angle so his 33,000-pound machine would be nearly parallel to the far, far larger vessel and only a foot or so from its solid steel, almost vertical hull. His two LVT crew members would then try to fend off any collision between the two hulls from the surging sea while, at the same time, keeping them close enough together so the men coming over the side of the ship could drop into the LVT instead of into the water between the two vessels. If they fell into the water, they would be crushed to death as the two hulls ground to and fro against each other.

The major made clear by repeated yelling and gestures that he and the other man wanted to board our LVT from near the stern of the destroyer on which they stood. The major may not have known this either, but his commands put him, his companion, and our LVT crew at far greater risk than even the dicey circumstances described above. The DE was close to the reef, and in a dangerous position herself. Should she begin to drift toward the reef with a change in the wind or wave pattern, her captain would almost certainly order her engines to turn her props to keep his ship off the reef, despite what any half-ass major might be doing on the stern of his ship. If the ship's captain had his engines rotate his props in reverse and we, in our LVT, were trying to board the major and his companion at the stern, we would almost certainly be sucked under and cut to pieces by the ship's propellers. With all this in mind and quite frightened, we managed to board the major and his companion without injury to anyone and with only a dented LVT hull and a damaged port-side track. Our hull was not breached. If we kept our track speed down, I estimated that we could avoid throwing that track and being helpless in the water.

I really hadn't had time to pay any attention to the major. He, by the way, had almost fallen into the sea between the LVT and the ship, wetting himself in the process. As soon as he settled his feathers, almost like a damp hen, he began giving orders, throwing spittle all the while. He said, "Lieutenant, you will carry us into the center of Red Beach, and at full speed."

There were two problems with these orders. First, the port track was damaged. If we operated it at full speed, we would almost certainly throw it off the forward drive sprocket and be helpless in the water. Second, the center of Red Beach was where we had just been earlier and barely survived. The Japs had tunneled into the interior of a fifteen or so foot high coral ridge just behind the beach and had emplaced 77mm high-velocity mountain guns. Burning and wrecked LVTs littered the reef. There were implanted beach mines as well, which destroyed additional LVTs. It was a mess. I tried to tell the major about these problems.

In addition, our port track was damaged on its outer retaining links, several steel links were broken. This put added strain on the inner links and tended to make the track deviate toward the hull. This was grossly obvious; it didn't take a genius to estimate what would happen if the track threw and jammed between the sprocket and the hull.

Further, a casual glance toward the center of Red Beach would have revealed a number of burning and/or blown up LVTs scattered on the reef, along with wounded men and floating bodies. Jap cannon fire might still be coming from their emplacements. If the major had been willing to look for himself, he could have seen all of this in a moment.

He declined to look, and, in his most officious manner said, "Lieutenant, be quiet. Do as you are told and be quick about it."

My crew and I were soaked with sea water, scared from having come a few minutes earlier within a hair of having been killed at just the place the major ordered us to land him and his companion, and thankful for having been spared, if only for a short while. I looked at him in resignation for a second, then started to turn to call through the hatch to our driver to head for the center of Red Beach.

I had been so focused on trying to keep our LVT from being disabled or sunk, helping our crew hold us a tolerable distance from the destroyer hull, avoiding injury to our crew and the two men we were boarding, and trying to tell the major of the extremely dangerous circumstances into which he was ordering us that I had paid little attention to the officer who was with him. At the moment I started to duck into the hatch to tell our driver to head for Hell again, the major's companion spoke to him. The companion's tone of voice was entirely different from that of the loud, blustery, officious tone of the major. The companion spoke to the major quietly, coolly and decisively, with well chosen and clearly enunciated words. He said, "Major, the lieutenant has just been into the middle of Red Beach. He knows his LVT. Let's listen to him."

I was so surprised that I just stared at him for a fraction of a second. In that fraction, I saw that he was a brigadier general and realized that he was Lemuel C. Shepherd, commanding officer of our First Provisional Marine Brigade, then composed of the Twenty-Second Regiment and the Raider regiment.

I saw in an instant the chance be had given me. First, I showed him our damaged left track and told him I estimated that if we turned our engine at about two-third speed in third gear, it might well hold. Further, I pointed out that there were no other undamaged LVTs near us into which we could transfer him and, still further, that such a transfer would take more time than our running him in ourselves. He looked at the track and looked about for any nearby LVTs. He looked back at me and smiled in recognition that I was alert to our situation and had already estimated our chances with some degree of experience and judgment. That smile also indicated that he valued my judgment and had some beginning trust in it.

With trust partly established, I then told him what my

crew and I had observed previously while crossing the reef and coming up on the beach to unload our troops. We had seen that just behind the center of Red Beach was the strongest point of the Jap defense.

In addition, I said, that defense was weaker at the south end of Red Beach. I explained that we had seen several of the Raiders head for that weak point just after they were landed by another one of our LVTs. They were certain to have dispatched any Japs then present. At that place was a tiny peninsula which had a few bushes on it, offering some cover. If we landed him there, I pointed out, he could work north a few hundred feet under cover so that he could soon be in his designated and expected position on shore.

He smiled again and said, "Do it." His wasn't the only smile. Our crewman who was manning the forward-mounted .50 caliber machine gun had a grin on his face that spread all the way across it.

I ducked into the hatch and told our driver to run at 1800 rpm engine speed in third gear, then shift down to first just before coming up on the reef. I would watch ahead and tell him just before we were to touch the coral. He and I coordinated this smoothly and correctly. We hauled out of the deep water onto the surface of the reef. After a few feet, the reef was smooth enough for our driver to shift into second and move fast enough to reduce our time in the exposed condition of crossing the wide reef.

We got over the reef without coming under further artillery or mortar fire and crawled up on the beach just at the south edge of the tiny peninsula. The major leaped out of the LVT, seven feet to the ground, and fell flat on his face in the sand. He got up and scuttled for cover in the bushes. General Shepherd climbed down over the side using the spaced foot holes. He reached up, smiled at us, shook hands, said "Thank you," and moved quietly into the ground cover.

I never saw him again. I will always remember his good judgment in grim circumstances, his command presence, his decency, and his gentlemanliness.

It was with deep pleasure that I learned, years later, that General Shepherd had been appointed Commandant of the Marine Corps.

From my experience with him, I doubt our nation could have found a better man.

Bad Ass

WE COMBAT LOADED for Guam at Tulagi and Guadalcanal. Our amphibian, tracked vehicles were driven up the ramp and through the bow doors onto the tank deck of an LST, an acronym for "Landing Ship, Tank." Our vehicle crews and the 300 or so marines we were to land in the first wave at Guam were boarded on the same, small ship.

Our men were packed below decks almost body to body. The tropical sun beating on the deck and hull of the ship, along with poor ventilation, made living conditions almost intolerable. Rotating men in shifts onto the open top deck was the only way we could ensure survival from day to day.

There was no fresh water for bathing or washing clothes; we were so short that drinking water was rationed. The water we did have was loaded at Tulagi and contaminated with fungus. Food was limited. Finally, the ship's cooks were reduced to baking bread from flour that was crawling with weevils. One just ate the baked larvae along with the rest of the bread.

Medical attention was provided by a corpsman, a person trained somewhat like a physician's assistant. The corpsman also served as a pharmacist. Despite everyone's best efforts, the ship soon stank of sweat, urine, and jungle ulcers.

This awful voyage lasted for 68 days.

We were short several men because of casualties sustained earlier. These wounded and killed-in-action men, whom we had served with in combat situations for months, had been comrades. Our casualties had been replaced by "brig rats," men who had been convicted of stealing, missing a ship going into combat, absence without leave, and other such offenses. We could not trust them. Going into combat with someone you cannot trust is at best a threat to any kind of organization and at worst an invitation to catastrophe.

Among these brig rats was a man who was a clear-cut danger to all of us. He was truly a Bad Ass.

One night our men came to me in desperation. I was the officer in charge of our LVT crews aboard ship. They knew, as I did, that we were going in the next couple of days into a perimeter-defended island whose defenders were in part Japanese Imperial Marines, some of the best troops the Japanese had and, to a man, fanatical fighters. We needed to be at our best. We had no slack to cut for anyone. It was do or die, probably both, for many of us.

The men wanted to talk with me about giving Bad Ass to Deep Six. This meant pushing him overboard at sea in the middle of the night. To those of you sitting at home with plenty of drinking water, a fresh shower, clean dry clothes and a full belly, this may seem an appalling and utterly unconscionable act. Under our desperate circumstances, it was an awful but not unreasonable attempt to resolve a coming situation which might cost all of us our lives.

I thought the matter over as best I could in the middle of the night on the tank deck as we wallowed along in a quartering sea at 10 or 11 knots. I told our men not to Deep Six him, just to watch him as best we could. None of us was satisfied. I agonized about it. Our people followed my orders.

One of the finest men I have ever known was my former platoon sergeant. His father had died a few months earlier, leaving him as the oldest son and the hope of his family. He was a man to whom honor, duty and responsibility came as naturally as breathing. He cared for his men and was respected by them. He had Bad Ass in his platoon.

Finally, our assault on the beach at Agat began. Before we could even crawl out of the water onto the coral sand beach, we were taken under fire by 77mm, high velocity, mountain artillery pieces which the Japanese had placed in caves just behind the beach. Our LVTs were loaded with mortar shells, flame-thrower material, and men. The men stood on loose boards atop the explosive load.

We were so close to the caves when the Japanese started firing that many of the 77mm artillery shells did not have time to rotate enough to arm their fuses before they hit the thin metal hulls of our LVTs. Some shells did arm; the LVTs these hit went up like skyrockets. Some of them set off underwater beach mines which the Japanese had laid.

A terrible time was had by all. Somehow, incomprehensibly, the platoon sergeant and his men survived that first day. After landing their troops they unloaded their cargo of mortar shells and flame-thrower materials and started removing the beach mines. One of the LVTs had hit a mine with its left track. The track, along with a bogie wheel, was blown off. Somehow, and I'll never know why, the LVTs hull was not breached by the mine blast, and its cargo did not detonate. Our men piled the 11-pound and larger 33-pound beach mines under the bow of the wrecked LVT after pulling them out of the sand and water. There were perhaps one hundred of these mines under the LVT. The stricken LVT was almost in the center of the platoon's sector. The sergeant backed his own LVT near the wrecked one so that he could direct his men in bringing in more marines, munitions, food, water and other materials. Wounded marines were transported back out to our ships.

Finally, night came and the Japs launched their expected counter-attack. Some of the Imperial Marines had wrapped layers of plastic explosive around their chests and bellies. In this soft, pliable explosive they had embedded hand grenades with the striker pin sticking out. They would come running in and set themselves off. Their jagged bone fragments were deadly shrapnel. One of them jumped onto the pile of mines under the knocked-out LVT and set it off. To say the least, there was a hell of a blast.

Fortunately, the platoon sergeant had moved his LVT

before nightfall and survived the explosion. I had hit something underwater coming into the beach with my LVT and had sheared off the left drive sprocket and track. I had waded ashore well before nightfall and was trying to coordinate the LVT company as best I could from a crater in the beach. Nothing hit me from the awful blast. I could see the platoon sergeant's LVT not far from my hole. I heard him calling to rally his men. He had the Bad Ass in the LVT with him so he could watch him.

One of his men was down, probably hit by some of the pieces of the blown up LVT. The platoon sergeant jumped from his LVT to see about his wounded man, leaving his driver and the Bad Ass in the LVT.

After a few moments of seeing to his wounded man, the platoon sergeant stood up to try to get the man a litter and help. At that point, Bad Ass took careful aim and shot the platoon sergeant and the wounded man both through the chest. I heard my friend and his man strangling on their own blood.

Fifty years later, I still agonize over my command decision not to Deep Six the Bad Ass. Would two fine men have survived and one rotten one died?

Viglio

VIG WAS A RUGGED, strong, solidly-built young man from New York City. Not only was he from the City, he had never been out of it or its suburbs until he enlisted in the Marine Corps, trained in boot camp, and was sent to us in Company A. Labile emotionally and with a short fuse, he was a fighter. Clearly, this was how he had learned to survive growing up in a tough neighborhood. Vig was bright. He didn't have much education but he knew how to prevail with street smarts.

Unlike other members of our company, he had almost no experience with mechanical equipment and showed little interest in learning the workings of our LVTs. Most of our men had a good bit of interest in internal combustion engines and machinery of one sort or another. They had grown up working on trucks, repairing broken vehicles and working with earth moving or road building equipment. They liked the work and had considerable skill in it and in learning more while they worked.

These features gave Vig problems. He was basically a decent fellow who was a fighter. This let him fit in with us, but not without considerable stress, which he exhibited by generalized tension and insistence, on his part, that the world he was in ought to be like the world in which he grew up, which it surely wasn't. Further, no amount of sneering at it was going to make it like he thought it ought to be.

He, and we, had little choice in all this administrative context. He was a member of our Company. He had to fit in whether he liked it or not.

What we, however, all had in common was an opportunity to experience the utterly different world we were in as an unfolding mystery, a wonderful chance to learn, a great adventure. Many of us were able to do this; it helped us laugh at and be tolerant of our thirst, hunger, isolation and exhaustion.

Vig didn't manage to generate this kind of experience. He lived with the vast emptiness of the sea, the isolation, the privation, as a heavy, constant burden. He compensated by building up more tension, until he was tight as an over-wound alarm clock and bitching constantly.

Viglio was like this when we arrived at our campsite at Guadalcanal. We built that camp in the middle of a malaria-ridden hell-hole called Tetere, about as different from New York City as one could imagine. We had a swamp pool at one side of our living area. It had blackish water alive with leeches. There was no other source of fresh water to bathe in except for a stagnant creek frequented by the truly dangerous estuarine crocodiles. Bathing there was dangerous. The thousand pound crocs would slip up under the surface without even a ripple, then come out of the water in a sudden rush too quick to avoid. Being taken by a croc was an awful risk. This left us the sea to bathe in. Those of you who have bathed in sea water to try to get clean know how miserable it is. The beach and sea water of our hell-hole had an added charm: there was a sunken ship just offshore which puked multiple globs of tarry Bunker C fuel oil at every change of tide. So we bathed, Vig among us, at the swamp pool and picked off the leeches before they could get their tooth-rimmed, spit-filled, bloodsucking mouths fixed in our flesh. Vig absolutely hated the leeches and would shudder when picking them off his skin.

His horror at the leeches was nothing, though, compared to his trembling and pallor at seeing his first, and every subsequent, tree alligator. None of us had experience with or knowledge of these great greenish arboreal lizards that inhabited trees shading our camp. We knew no name for the four-foot long egg eaters that leaped from tree to tree in long jumps like great, scaly, greenish squirrels. We called them tree alligators. Vig was frozen with terror at just seeing one climbing about in the trees above him. He began to be unable to contain his stress. He was headed for trouble.

As usual, many of us had diarrhea. We had been fortunate, in that someone had managed to steal from the dog faces (army) several large bolts of unbleached, muslin-like cloth. We used this to build an enclosed, tent-like privy. Since we would spend much of our time there, the construction was done with care. The cloth would help a bit in keeping the flies off our excrement and give us some relief from their solicitous attention.

Of course, we had no electricity. We went to bed at sunset and, except for getting up in the night for diarrheal stools, arose at first light in the morning. Again, someone, both creative and light-fingered, had liberated a gasoline lantern. We fueled it, pumped it up, lit it at dusk, and hung it in our brand new, cloth-walled privy. Its harsh, bright light caused the off-white cloth to glow in the dark as a beacon for the diarrhea-stricken marines, rushing to make it to the privy. If you were sick and about to soil yourself, it was truly a Guiding Light.

Our first night with the lantern, we went to sleep with the comforting knowledge that we could see to get to the can in a hurry. That same first night, Vig had diarrhea. He started out for the glowing, lighted privy. He was sleepy, his senses dulled, and half sick. Vig rushed into the privy, sat down, and emitted with an abdominal cramp a huge, bubbling, wet stool with immense relief. Then he looked about him. The rather large, four-hole privy was dirt-floored. Attracted by the light and climbing all over each other were dozens and dozens of tree alligators. They were looking at Vig with their cold, staring, reptilian eyes and flicking in and out their glistening, reddish-purple, long, split tongues. They crawled over Vig's feet and legs with a rasping, cold, scaly slithering. He was near ass-deep in arboreal alligators. There was a piercing, agonistic, lost-soul scream. It woke almost everyone in camp. Vig ran right through the side of the brand new privy, tearing the cloth apart. He continued to let out awful wails as he ran away. His eyes had become partly accustomed to the bright light from the lantern. He could see nothing in the dark. He didn't run far before he hit a tree, knocking him flat. Vig was lying on the ground with a bloody head and yelling wildly when we got to him. We had to—several of us—pin him down by holding each arm and leg. He continued to struggle and yell for perhaps fifteen minutes untill he was too exhausted to do much more than breathe in sobbing gasps.

We stayed with him the rest of the night, a long one indeed. By sunup Vig had settled down a bit physically and was not struggling, just babbling incoherently.

We carried him off to a navy medical outfit where they sedated him. He was acutely psychotic. After a time the navy people arranged for him to be sent back to the States.

Do you suppose that had Vig made a deep decision many months before to experience all that was so totally foreign to him as a fascinating, unfolding mystery instead of an uncontrollable, crushing burden that all of this might have been a wonderful and growthful adventure for him instead of a psychotic horror? It might have been.

It wasn't.

Hospitalization

WE HAD MANY seriously wounded marines in the landing on the beach at Agat. The 77mm cannon fire from the Japanese sent an awful lot of jagged metal flying through the air. Amputated or near-amputated limbs were frequent amongst our men. These people were brought to a central, semi-secure location just behind the beach. Three tents were hastily erected, one for a surgical arena, one for a ward of marines with head, chest and abdominal wounds and a third for men with amputations of legs and/or arms.

At best, this was a gory mess, probably beyond your imagination. I went there because some of my men were there. I wanted to tell them that I cared for them and that I thanked them for their courage and sacrifice. I was hardly prepared for what I found.

By sheer luck, a tent had been erected over a Japanese cache of several bottles of sake. Loose dirt covered the bottles initially. As more and more non-amputee corpsmen brought in more and more litters with wounded men, the corpsmen's boots gradually scraped the dirt from the bottles so that they could be seen. One of the marines with a good arm and hand reached off his canvas cot and began to dig with his fingers. There was a stunned silence for a few moments as the four or five bottles of sake were uncovered. Then a great whoop of joy went up. The bottles were opened and the rice wine shared amongst the twenty-five or so wounded men in the tent. At five men to a bottle, there was certainly not enough to get anyone drunk, so the ensuing fight could not be blamed on drunkenness. It was so psychotically awful as to be incomprehensible at first. Men with amputated legs were trying to kick each other with the stumps, breaking open the surgical repairs, with blood and gore spattering in every direction. Those with arm wounds were punching anybody in sight, whether they had fists or not.

To a man, everyone was laughing until tears ran down their faces, tears of joy. Each had, in honor, a ticket. Each had paid for that ticket with his blood. Each had a ticket out of Hell.

Dengue Fever

WE HAD A HELL of a mess at our "Home on the Range" campsite at Agat Beach, Guam (figure 9). Our few tents were ragged and torn, offering only limited protection from rain or sun and almost nothing from anything else. Most of us were sleeping on the ground underneath the bows of our LVTs. When the engine of the vehicle was started unexpectedly or in an emergency, there was a wild scramble to get out from under the vehicle's cleated tracks to avoid being crushed and cut to pieces.

We had no netting, insect repellant, or other means of protection from mosquitoes. Those mosquitoes were present in intensely hungry hordes. Hundreds of thousands of them hadn't had food in a long time. To call them "ravenous" in their search for a taste of our blood is an understatement; our faces and hands were swollen from bites on top of other bites. We were bitten through our clothing as well. There was no one of us who was not bitten time after time, often hundreds of times.

Dengue fever is believed to be caused by a virus borne by mosquitoes. Surviving the illness is associated with long term, subsequent immunity. There had been, during the lives of our young men, no widespread outbreaks of dengue in the United States. Few of our men, reared in the time of the Great Depression, had ever had the money or opportunity to live in any other country and almost no one had even heard of dengue fever. Our immunity to infection with the dengue virus must have been near zero.

Several days after our landing at Agat Beach, and in a single twenty-four to thirty-six hour period, at least one-half of our people came down with a devastating febrile illness. There was prostration, extreme weakness, a terrible deep-seated pain in one's body, and a kind of behind the eyes, crushing headache that was like nothing I had ever experienced before and have never since. This eye and skull pain was so intense that I could not tolerate moving my eyes in their sockets. To change my field of vision, I had to turn my head or move my entire body. We had a number of our people who had a rash of mild to moderate degree. Thank goodness, we had no one with a massive hemorrhagic rash and shock.

Within another day or so after the first cases, almost every one of us was sick. We had no doctor. We did have a navy medical corpsman at that time. He had a single, mercury-type, glass thermometer. This was put to more use in a few days than its designers had estimated that it would be used in its entire lifetime.

The corpsman would go around each morning and take oral temperatures. Anyone with a fever of less than 104 degrees F was considered well enough to work. Those with fever above 104 degrees *F* were taken off duty and moved to shady areas to rest. On one of these days I had a bit lower than 104 degrees *F* and was working with men at least as sick as I was to get as many as possible of our LVTs in shape to operate. I was standing on the seven-foot tall stern of a non-running LVT in order to examine its engine. I stood up and was so weak that I fell off the LVT into the mud hole shown in the lower corner of Fig. 9. I was too weak to get out and just lay in the slop.

In today's world, as you read these words, what I have told you may well seem beyond belief, brutal and negligent. What I hope you will understand is that we were in a terrible situation with no help available and none that we had the power to make available. We had to continue to fight the Japanese.

Even if we had had a doctor we could turn to, that doctor almost certainly would have had no experience in treating people with what was then known in many tropical countries as "Breakbone Fever." Even if the doctor had, by some outside chance, ever seen a case before, there was nothing definitive that he could have done. The issue had already been joined between us and the virus. We would either survive or die.

Before we were ever exposed to dengue virus, we had had many weeks of little food, exposure to the elements, bouts of diarrhea and constant demands for repeated combat operations. Our men were ill-nourished, thin, weakened, and exhausted. How we survived this illness is a miracle. It is one for which, to this day, I am deeply thankful and still surprised.

Every one of us lived.

All in a Day's Work

WE HAD A BLOODY landing at Agat, a village near the base of the Orote Peninsula at Guam. The Japanese had a beach defense and a rearward defense with observation posts on the high ground just inland from the town.

Our LVTs had been hard hit with point-blank 77mm flat trajectory gunfire from emplacements just behind the beach. The marines we landed were from the Raider Regiment and the 22nd Marine Regiment. They stood in the open-top LVTs on loose boards that overlaid a foot-thick layer of mortar shells. It was bad.

One of the battalions we landed was commanded by a major, a man who, through his bravery and capacity for leadership, had been commissioned in the field from the noncommissioned officer ranks. I had worked with him in the past in a complex reconnaissance in the atolls of the southern Marshall Islands and knew him personally to be an experienced, capable, fine man. In his battalion and under his command was another, quite different, but also fine man. This was a young fellow, about 18, from Tennessee. He was not long out of boot camp. He was scared, but never shirked. He was a decent young man who never broadcast or insisted upon his religion but deeply believed in it. He carried his Bible in his pack. His fellow marines respected and cared for him, particularly since he was a powerful man physically and was perfectly willing to fight and set on their collective asses those who weren't.

His company was not as hard hit in our landing as some of the others. He and most of his mates survived, as did the major.

After a day or so, our people began to advance along the base of the Orote Peninsula to cut it off from the Japanese troops on the rest of the island. The Japanese resisted tenaciously and made a night attack on the area where the young Tennessee man's company had dug in for the night with hastily scraped-out foxholes in the rotted coral rock. The Japanese attacked with tanks in one area while individual Nips slipped toward our people's foxholes to kill them quietly.

A Japanese got in the foxhole with the young Tennessee man, whose attention was directed toward the tanks and associated advancing troops. He slit the young man's throat so he could not call out an alarm. Then, inexplicably, the Japanese proceeded to cut off the young man's penis, scrotum and testicles. Even less understandably, he stayed in the hole with the bled-out young man until daylight. He was still there with the man's penis and testicles in his hand when our people found him.

The young man's mates were so wildly infuriated by what they found that they proceeded to cut the Japanese into strips, leaving only the bones held together by ligaments, cartilage and bits of muscle. They then threw the still-articulated skeleton into the road, where it would be run over by the vehicular traffic. A League of Nations observer, Red Cross worker, or noncombatant of some kind, saw the latter part of this and reported it. It took a few days, but then a great investigation was initiated. Eventually, the battalion commanding officer, the major, was court-martialed.

In sum, the major was ruined, the young man was emasculated, the Japanese was cut into strips and the reporting non-combatant went psychotic.

Some days things just don't go right at all.

Quick Wit

IT HAD RAINED almost steadily for two days. The earth had absorbed all the water it could. Our paths and dirt trails were muddy and slippery.

There is a kind of Philippine water buffalo known as *carabao*. These are large, wide-bodied, sway-backed, smooth-haired domesticated animals weighing perhaps as much as a ton or more. Usually docile, they seem to adore immersing themselves in bog holes that are part water, part mud, and part slime. Their wallowing and rolling about is so ecstatically joyful to the carabao that they, using the polite term, often relieve themselves. The result, as you can understand, is a foul mess.

Past one of these wallow pits came two of our men—wet, miserable and ill-tempered. One of them slipped and fell in, fully immersing himself in the awful, stinking, semi-liquid.

He came to the surface sputtering and gasping for breath. As he started to climb out, coated with mud and dripping slime, he saw his buddy standing on the path above him, laughing. This lit his fuse and he went wild. He hauled himself back up onto the slick path, stood up and started cursing his laughing friend. Saying words that I will not repeat here, he ended his rant with the statement, "And you rotten bastard, you can kiss my ass!"

In no more than a fraction of a second came the reply from his friend in a falsely solicitous tone: "Of course I will. Just smile to give me a clue."

Decorations and Medals

AS I HAVE told you, we had a bloody time in the assault on Guam. Our landing vehicles landed the Raider Regiment and the 22nd Regiment in the first and following waves at Agat near the base of the Orote Peninsula. Our LVTs were heavily loaded with a layer of mortar shells next to the steel deck. On top of the mortar shells were loose boards, called "dunnage." The men stood on the boards and the mortar shells.

As one can imagine, a shell fired at point-blank range and penetrating the beer-can-thick hull of an LVT heaving out of the water and climbing onto the beach did heavy damage. Burning and exploding LVTs lay in the knee-deep water covering the fringing coral reef, and they littered the beach.

John David was a giant, dark-haired and tan-skinned platoon leader in my LVT outfit. Our friend, John Wilson, called John David a "dark Irishman," the first time I, a sheltered Southern boy, had ever heard the term. John David was immensely courageous. He lost four of the five LVTs in his under-strength platoon, all except his. In the midst of withering cannon and small arms fire, he leaped out of his seven-foot-high LVT into the knee-deep sea water cover-

Figure 8. The author, wearing one of the shirts given him by the colonel.

Figure 9. Home on the Range. Our camp at Agat Beach.
(Photo courtesy of Harold Gaebe)

ing the reef. He waded, in turn, to each of his four disabled and burning vehicles. On his shoulders, sometimes two at a time, he carried grievously wounded marines to his own LVT—the only one that was still running. There is no accurate count of how many men he saved from near-certain death.

John David never got a scratch in all this. Not only that, he previously had played four years of college football at a college in Pennsylvania with tough coal miners. He never got hurt. Wilson, who was witness to some of this, got blown up and out of his LVT by a Japanese, one-tit beach mine. His one comment on John David's not being hit was, "The son of a bitch is charmed."

We all marveled at John David's charmed nature. I fully expected the commanding officer to put him up for the Congressional Medal of Honor.

With this in mind, I was not surprised when the C.O. called John David in to his command post several days later. For whatever reason, I happened to be there at that time to see the colonel about getting vehicle spare parts. John David and I went in together. The colonel looked John David square in the eyes. He said, "Lieutenant, you did well. Here are two shirts . . . and here's two for you too, Sciple."

We left. The matter was never mentioned again.

Incomprehensible

MY MIND, NO matter how I tried, could not grasp the Jap manner of being. It was, and is, utterly beyond me. I will give you a single example that I hope will help you understand my lack of understanding.

The watch that I am wearing now is a third generation descendant of the one that I took off the left wrist of a headless lieutenant of marines who had made his first, and only, fatal mistake just behind the beach where we had landed his platoon of riflemen at Roi-Namur, Kwajalein Atoll. He had stuck his head above the sill of a palm log Jap emplacement from which they had been firing at us as we hauled up out of the water in the first wave of the assault. Our LVT .50 caliber machine gunners had managed to fire through the embrasure of the sturdy palm log bunker, killing all but one of the Japs manning the automatic weapon emplaced within it. One Jap was still alive and active within the bunker. He had a cylindrical, serrated-surface grenade stuffed in his mouth with the brass strike pin and fuse tip facing outward. He struck the pin and activated the several second fuse. This gave him time to rise up to, and then above, the level of the sill. He grabbed the lieutenant by the neck and held his head and the marine's head together. The grenade exploded, blowing off both their heads at neck level.

My watch had been sea-water soaked during our trip to the beach and was useless. I had to have a working watch so I unfastened my wrist strap, took off the wet watch, similarly unfastened the lieutenant's strap, took off his watch, put mine on his wrist and his on mine. It worked fine. It made no difference to him since he had nothing to see with anyway.

With this background, you can understand why I was chary of coming close to the slant-eyed bastards unless it was clear that they were good, solid dead. Others of our people had seen the grenade-in-the-mouth trick as well. It was a not uncommon action on their part; whether they had been taught this in their training, I never knew.

Much later, in the Marianas Islands, I was at a place where five or six captured Japs were being herded into a barbed-wire enclosure. We seldom captured any of them and were not practiced and skillful at handling them. We learned later to strip them naked, search their clothes and let them redress before turning them free inside the barbed-wire pen.

One of the several slant-eyes suddenly pulled a grenade out of his pants, stuffed it into his mouth, pushed in the striker pin and grabbed by the neck an incautious marine standing next to him. The grenade fuse had been wet and the explosive did not detonate. The Jap looked surprised for a second, let go of the transfixed marine's neck, spit out the grenade, bowed slightly, smiled at his new friend and said, in excellent English: "Got a cigarette, Mac?"

Incomprehensible.

Martinet

WHEN OUR LOST Company was dissolved, a number of our men and I were transferred to an LVT battalion which happened to be camped near our then-abandoned Company A camp. We had never had contact with the people of this battalion and had never worked with them in a combat situation. They were not particularly pleased to have attached to them a group of ragged, half-sick, worn-out marines. It was a less than happy union. They had no great supply of shoes, clothing, toilet articles or other things we lacked. Not only had they no excess, they were less than interested in sharing what they did have, considering us a bit like uninvited and unwanted squatters.

We were not a pretty sight and certainly not a spit and polish outfit. Our shoes were held together with twine or bits of insulation-stripped copper telephone wire, our dungarees were worn to the point where great jagged holes were present in them. Many of our men were sick with hepatitis and obviously jaundiced, with yellowed eyes and skin. We had no fresh razor blades and were shaved in only the roughest manner. We had one of us who acted as a barber. He had no skill and only a pair of broken scissors to use in cutting our hair. In sum, we were a sorry looking bunch of burnt-out marines. We needed—and needed badly—water, food, clothes, bathing facilities, medical care, and rest.

The battalion into which we had been transferred was attached to a marine division which had lost its second in command. A colonel, up for promotion to brigadier, was sent from Marine Corps School in Quantico, Virginia to replace him. The colonel was a rigid, demanding, small-minded man who had been stateside in an academic and ceremonial environment for so long that he had either forgotten, or perhaps had never known, what prolonged combat and privation were really like. If somehow he did know, he had no respect for the results of these in his system of values.

About three or four days after our transfer, we got word that this gentleman, the assistant division commander, was to hold an inspection. Not only was he to hold an inspection, he was to hold it that same afternoon. We had just time enough to get our men out onto a burned-over field and in formation when the colonel arrived. He had some kind of an executive officer with him, along with a perfectly uniformed, laundered, pressed and spotless sergeant major. They were accompanied by a command car driver and two flunkies to take notes.

With all the various companies in the battalion to choose from, the colonel headed for our ragged people like a vulture diving on its rotting prey. He stopped before me. As the senior officer—a first lieutenant—of our ragged and quite motley group, I was posted alone and in front of our men, all lined up and standing at attention. He looked me over at first with surprise, this soon turning to disgust and confusion. He may never before have seen a marine officer in such a mess. His expression slowly turned into one of great relief. He knew how to deal with this slovenliness, this threat to his sense of the essential orderliness of his world, regardless of its origin. He should, could and would move at once with all his authority to restore this Breach of Good Order and Discipline.

Starting in on me as a warm up for his afternoon accomplishment, he ordered me to empty my map case. I never knew why he seized on this utterly useless and unimportant piece of equipment—possibly because it looked brand new and unused, which it was. I had not used it except at inspections. We never had any maps anyway. Even if we had had maps, they would have been soaked by sea water and useless if I had carried them around in that damn case.

In this military administrator's mind, the field officer's map case was some kind of Holy Grail, to be observed and appraised at every inspection. Mine got in my way and I kept it hidden except for inspections. This was a cardinal sin, soon to be revealed and publicly punished.

As ordered, I emptied my map case. Since there was no bench or table, I turned it upside down and poured its contents on the ground at my feet There were, of course, no maps. Out fell sixteen .45 caliber pistol rounds and a partly eaten K-ration fruit bar which I had been saving for an emergency meal. The colonel's disgust turned to fury. His whole sense of the world and its proper order had been violated. This was a time for punishment. He ordered me to remove my steel helmet. My hair was long and shaggy. He seized on this and ordered me to have all the men I commanded remove their helmets so that he could inspect haircuts. Of all unimportant things to seize upon in a situation of great deprivation, this may have been the least significant.

I had never heard the command "Uncover, two!" the correct one for removing headgear. I proceeded to tell our men, still at attention, "The colonel will inspect haircuts; remove your helmets." This ignorance on my part angered the colonel yet again. He responded by berating me in front of my men in a really vicious manner. He ordered me to accompany him while he inspected, found fault with, and degraded each of our men. He had his flunkies take notes on all this.

Fortunately I was able, just barely, to keep myself in check. To abuse our men and me in this cheap, two-bit manner infuriated me almost beyond my being able to contain that fury. I wanted to grab this stinking son of a bitch and stuff his head so far up his rotten ass that his cries for help could be heard only as a distant, wet echo.

What our men deserved and needed was a "Well done" and a kept promise of clean water, clothes, shoes, food and rest.

They never got it from this incompetent martinet.

Bobby Lee

BOBBY LEE WAS a worthless bastard.

He came to our outfit straight from boot camp. He had distinguished himself there by lying, malingering, stealing, and skillfully slipping out of work details.

In peacetime, he would have been thrown out of the Marine Corps within a few weeks after enlisting. The desperation of our national position after the Japanese sneak attack on Pearl Harbor was so extreme that Bobby Lee was kept on duty.

His record book, of course, came with him when he was detailed to us. One look at it convinced our first sergeant that there was no good administrative means of getting rid of Bobby Lee, and second, that we were almost certain to have trouble on our hands in keeping him. As was often the case, the first sergeant was right, right on both counts.

Before too long, though, Bobby Lee did us an unexpected favor. In our training at Courthouse Bay, we had some associated Coast Guard people who were working with us on coordinating the use of small vessels with our tracked, amphibious vehicles. The coasties' vessels were probably about twenty feet in length and had a hull that would plane on the water surface when the vessel was not loaded and its engine was run wide open. Some were powered by two-cy-cle, GM, diesel engines, about which there was little good to say. Two, however, were powered by immense Hall-Scott, V-8 gasoline engines. These two boats would run like scald-ed dogs. They were fitted with twin, three-inch diameter, stainless steel, water-cooled, exhaust pipes. When operated at full throttle, they had a deep, roaring, rumbling sound that brought lust to the heart of a psychopath. Bobby Lee listened. He lusted.

One Saturday night well after dark, we heard the un-mistakable roar of one of those Hall-Scotts starting up. With no warm-up period, the man at the throttle pushed it full to the firewall and started away from our dock at flank speed. The passage from the dock to the deeper waters of the in-let was narrow, shallow and difficult to negotiate, even in broad daylight. Through the grace of an incoming tide and a hull almost out of the water from the immense power of the Hall-Scott, the boat made it the quarter-mile or so out to deeper water. The exhaust roar in the quiet night could be heard for miles. We listened and could tell that the pilot was headed for Oyster Landing, several miles across the in-let. In that day, Oyster Landing had a few unpainted wood-en houses, electric lights, dirt roads, no telephones, and a restaurant. This latter was equipped with saw-board tables, benches, a tin roof, and a cranky old proprietor who didn't like marines. After this night, he would have good reason to like them even less.

Bobby Lee wanted beer. He had decided to steal a Browning Automatic Rifle just before he stole the Hall-Scott-powered boat. After these two thefts, he planned further Saturday night fun. He landed near the Oyster Restaurant after crossing the several-mile-wide inlet. Carrying the BAR, a formidable weapon, he entered the restaurant by kicking in the door when all he needed to do to get inside was to turn the doorknob. He took the cranky old proprietor prisoner, tied him hand and foot, robbed him and then threatened to burn him alive to force him to tell where he kept the beer. Bobby Lee got $14, all there was in the money box. He found two cases of beer. He carried the beer to the boat, started the engine so as to make a quick getaway, and returned to set the building on fire. As he was starting to set the fire, he heard a truck coming. Out of pure meanness, he slashed the old man laterally across the chest before running to the stolen boat.

The occupants of the truck never saw Bobby Lee. They did see the newly-started fire and ran to put it out. They found the proprietor tied hand and foot with a long, bloody chest wound showing through his dirty, slit shirt. Bobby Lee's knife had struck ribs but had not penetrated the inner chest wall to the lungs beneath. He was bleeding, but fully able to speak and tell what had happened.

Much earlier, when we heard the boat engine start and then followed the engine roar by ear, we suspected that the thief was Bobby Lee and that his target was the restaurant.

Since there was no phone, we could not warn the old man. We sent out an armed party which arrived by road well after Bobby Lee had left. Our people loaded the bleeding man into their vehicle and carried him to the hospital.

Before they could get to a telephone and call us, Bobby Lee had gotten back across the inlet. We were waiting for him. As he was unloading the beer onto the dock, our men jumped him. His BAR, thank goodness, fell into the water where we later recovered it—still loaded and ready to fire.

In the wild struggle in the dark, Bobby Lee got his hand on the throttle, pushed it full on and leaped from the boat. Three of our men were in the boat with a wide-open throttle and no helmsman. One man was still on the dock. He thought Bobby Lee was one of his squad members and let him get away. Bobby Lee ran up the dock with the $14 but without the stolen beer, later said to have fallen in the water and been "not recovered." In the confusion, Bobby Lee got away. He found a 1938 Plymouth 4-door automobile owned by one of the coast guard chief petty officers. It had the keys in the ignition lock and a full tank of gas. Bobby Lee started it and lit out for our entrance road, which led to the road system for the rest of the vast Camp Lejeune base.

We had a guardhouse at the road junction. The MP on duty signaled for the car to stop. Bobby Lee's response was to floorboard the accelerator pedal and steer straight for the MP, striking him a glancing blow as the man leaped for safety. Another MP fired his weapon at the fast-disappearing rear of the Plymouth. He did not hit Bobby Lee, but put several rounds through the chief's pride and joy, ventilating it rather fully.

Before long, and while still recovering from their near-death experience, the MPs heard a racing engine not far away. They reloaded their weapons and got ready for another pass-through. This time the sound stayed in the same place. Bobby Lee had run into a ditch and was stuck. We sent out another armed party with orders to get him, dead or alive. Unfortunately, they brought him back alive. He was court-martialed, convicted and sent to the naval prison in Portsmouth. We thought we were through with the son of a bitch for once and for all. This was not to be.

Two years later, overseas and after several combat operations, we had lost many of our men. The losses had made men trained in the use of our tracked, amphibious, tank-like vehicles a hot commodity. The Marine Corps ranks were scoured for such people. They found Bobby Lee in the naval prison, paroled him and sent him to us at Guam as "rehabilitated." He was about as welcome in our grim circumstances as a roach in a punch bowl. We had no time to fool with the likes of him. Our people, some of them, knew him from long before. They despised Bobby Lee and cut him no slack, not even an inch. We watched him closely. About all we noticed was that he kept a large, white sheet of graph paper with him. He made marks on it from time to time. This made us no trouble so we left him alone; we just didn't have the time or energy to look into the matter.

The Guamanian people, Chamorros, were at that time not U.S. citizens, as best I understood it. They were termed U.S. nationals and were under the protection of our government. They had been wonderfully loyal to the United States during the Japanese occupation of Guam. Our people held them in the highest regard. Even a minor transgression against them by a marine was a matter of great consequence. It called for severe punishment. No such punishment had occurred, to my knowledge, since we all got along together quite well indeed. Most of us thought the world and all of these wonderful people.

Bobby Lee had been a bit more than a month with us. One night he slipped away without anyone knowing he was gone. A Chamorro family down the road from our camp was having an extended family ceremony and feast. They had repaired the collateral damage to their *fale* (house) and had even managed to replace their former thatched roof with corrugated metal sheets, what I had always called "roofing tin." A roofing tin roof was a mark of social distinction amongst the village people. They had a great deal to celebrate and were doing it in style. The party was to last all day and all night, with various ceremonies, feasting, orations, incantations, dancing and music. There were probably twenty or so people present. It was a joyous time for them. In the midst of this, Bobby Lee slipped out of the dark and into the gathering in the house. He grabbed a young girl, tore off her clothes near the doorway and started to rape her while, at the same time, threatening to shoot with his pistol the stunned family members if they so much as moved a muscle. While he was having his way with the girl, he was distracted enough for a young man to jump out a window and drop to the ground undetected. This young fellow ran to our camp. We gathered a party, all armed, and moved quietly down the road. We surrounded the house, each picking a window or door. We burst in just as Bobby Lee was starting to rape a second Chamorro girl. We took him without firing a shot or injuring a single member of the Chamorro family. We hog-tied him and dragged him off, face down.

The incident started a great administrative turmoil and investigation. Bobby Lee's personal effects were examined in detail. His sheet of white graph paper was located. When looked at carefully, it was found to be a kind of calendar on which he had been marking off each day of his parole. His last parole day was the day before he went to the Chamorro party. As we grasped it, he was waiting to get off parole before starting his old tricks again.

An even more careful look at his marking sheet and a comparison with his parole papers revealed an error. Bobby Lee had miscounted his days and was still on his last day of parole. He left us in handcuffs, waist chain, leg irons, and under the tender care of two armed platoon sergeants.

Never give a psychopath a second chance.

Non-psychotic, Organic Brain Syndrome Etiology: Repeated Head Trauma

WE HAD A BETTER name for it. We called it Squash Rot.

Andy had the bad Squash Rot. He wasn't completely destroyed intellectually. He could dress himself, eat without help, keep more or less clean and talk in simple sentences. But as one of our men put it, "He sure as hell isn't right." It didn't take a genius to tell that.

Andy had survived an appalling series of injuries and mishaps. He had been in his Amtrac on a reef at New Georgia in the Solomons north of Guadalcanal. He was headed for the beach and out of the open sea. He had crawled up onto an old, rotted, dead-coral reef. His driver was moving slowly with good traction in a few inches of water. Andy was watching closely ahead of him for deep pockets with just-underwater coral heads.

Just above the bushes fringing the beach came a single engine Jap naval aircraft. The pilot was flat on the deck at no more than twenty feet altitude. Under his left wing dangled a small bomb left over from an earlier run elsewhere. Its tail fins were fouled on the release mechanism. The slant-eye saw Andy and, in a split second, realized that he was so low his prop wouldn't clear the seven-foot-tall Amtrac. He jerked back on his stick and went into a full-power climb. This sudden maneuver dislodged the hanging bomb. It skipped across the shallow water over the reef and detonated under the hull of Andy's LVT. His driver and gunner were killed. Andy was blown up into the air out of the open LVT. He landed in a few inches of water on the reef. That water and the loose, rotted coral particles just under the water almost surely saved his life.

Our people reached him in a few moments before he could drown. With a great deal of good sense, they got a large board that had been blown out of the LVT along with Andy. They eased the board under the semiconscious man while he was still lying in, and partly supported by, the sea water. They tied his hips, legs, head and arms to the board. They heard his deep, coarse breathing—often present in people with brain injuries—and realized that any ties around his chest might limit that breathing and cause him to die just as they were trying to save him.

With considerable skill, perhaps born of necessity, they eased Andy up the seven-foot-high sides of an undamaged LVT and into its open cargo compartment. They drove him back over the reef to the sea and then out to an old, battered ship which was serving as a floating first aid station. Still strapped to the board, he was hoisted up out of the bobbing LVT, its hull banging in the waves against the hull of the ship, and onto the ship's deck. A doctor looked Andy over in a quick examination. He was semiconscious, had no open head wound, but was oozing clear, straw-colored spinal fluid from his nose and both ears. This is an ominous sign. It indicates that there has been a skull fracture with displacement great enough to produce meningeal tears and underlying damage to brain tissue. An immediate risk, if no massive brain injury, is that of bacterial infection. The bacteria can pass from the nose and ears through the meningeal tears and into the pan-cerebral fluid. A bacterial meningitis may result.

There was nothing to do for Andy but to keep him still and quiet, with the hope that he would not develop meningitis and would not have lethal swelling of his brain from the trauma he had undergone. They did not give him fluids. If he survived a few hours, his kidneys would hopefully produce enough urine to dehydrate him a bit and possibly draw fluid from his blood and help with the brain swelling. This was before the days of antibiotics and the doctors could only hope for no bacterial meningitis. In the absence of meningitis and of massive cerebral edema (swelling), it was clear that the longer Andy lived, the greater were his chances of continuing to live.

He was placed below decks in a small compartment with several other injured marines. That compartment happened to be almost exactly at the water line on the hull of the ship. Andy's litter was placed next to the hull and several feet above the compartment's deck, with another litter and another wounded marine beneath him.

After dark, the battered ship set sail for the field hospital back at Guadalcanal, where better care could be given to the wounded men. Several hours into that voyage, the vessel was taken under attack by a Jap submarine. The submarine launched a torpedo which apparently porpoised in and out of the water several times before hitting the first-aid ship almost exactly at the water line. Had the warhead fired, this would have been the end of the story.

The warhead did not fire, but the torpedo was so heavy and coming so fast that it penetrated the rusty hull of the old ship. That penetration was into Andy's compartment, nearly knocking him off his litter and soaking him with sea water. The compartment lights stayed on. There was a 2000-pound, 10-foot long torpedo, its warhead intact, lying on the deck with its engine hissing steam and its propellers spinning wildly. It lay there the rest of the night. Sailors gently shored it up against the bulkheads and packed it in blankets with the hope that there would not be enough rolling or vibration of the ship to set off the several-hundred-pound warhead. Can you imagine what it would be like in these terrible circumstances?

The United States was in a desperate part of our desperate struggle with the Japanese. We, in the Amtracs, had taken heavy losses. We needed every man we could get. After a long, forward area hospitalization, Andy was sent to us as "fit for duty." Whoever made that medical determination was the ultimate optimist, no matter how badly we needed replacements. Andy was near helpless. He could, and would, follow simple, direct instructions. That wasn't enough. We were preparing for yet another operation where we would be landing against the Imperial Marines. We had to depend on each other if any of us were to live. We could not depend on Andy. He had long since given his best, no matter what any dimwitted administrative opinion might be to the contrary.

By this time, we were at Guam. We had a tent camp along the shore north of the ruined city of Agana. A short way from us, up a dirt road, was a Quonset hut naval hospital, just being built and open for patients for only a few days. They owed us a favor. We had driven some Japanese away after they had run through the hospital area in the middle of the night, firing, throwing grenades and generally raising hell.

We saw our chance and called in our chit. We dressed Andy in rumpled khakis and gave him a pith helmet to accentuate his vacant stare. We made up a cock-and-bull story of Andy's having had a seizure and repeated it to him so many times that he came to believe it himself. He could repeat it at least fairly convincingly without prompting. We led him, with his wrinkled clothing, pith helmet, vacant stare and story of a seizure, into the admitting area of the hospital. The navy captain commanding the hospital passed the word about Andy after we explained to him that the Japs were still in the jungle nearby and that he might need us again, perhaps even that very night. It worked. Andy was admitted for observation and an indeterminate stay. It worked better than we had foreseen. The nurse in charge of Andy's ward took an instant interest in him that rapidly grew in intensity and intimacy. Andy was not too far gone to respond.

One Sunday afternoon Andy and the nurse got a Jeep from somewhere. They drove off into the bush a considerable distance from the hospital. They went down a trail in the middle of nowhere to a little turnaround, fully believing that they were alone. They got out of the Jeep and began making passionate love on the almost flat engine hood. The hood was hot, but so were they. They never noticed three Japanese in tattered uniforms who suddenly appeared out of the bush. One of them threw a grenade which rolled along the ground and lodged at the sidewall of the tire on the left front wheel of the vehicle. It detonated. Fortunately, much of the force and shrapnel went into the tire and steel wheel. Andy and the nurse, locked in a copulatory embrace and at orgasm, were blown off the hood as a united pair. The Japanese ran off.

Andy and his companion were stunned and badly shaken up, having no idea of what had happened, never having experienced a gigantic orgasm like this one. Neither sustained any shrapnel wounds. Both were temporarily deafened. They drove back to the hospital in low, low gear at about three mph on a bent and shrapnel-scarred steel wheel, with no tire. Their flimsy account was that they had hit a small anti-personnel mine in the open road and had detonated it.

The captain in command of the hospital did not believe the story, since the evidence really didn't fit well. He was also less concerned than he had been about the hospital's security and didn't need our protection like he had previously. He had just gotten in some MPs who could stand guard at night.

Andy became a solvable problem for the captain. Clearly, Andy's hospital days were numbered. He certainly was no better after the Sunday picnic, but he wasn't a great deal worse than he had been. In a few days, he was returned to us as "fit for duty." Our attempt to subvert the system in a decent cause had failed: failed for Andy, failed for the rest of us.

We were combat-loading our ships for the landing at Iwo. Our company was broken up to fill in other companies that were under-strength.

The last time I saw Andy, he had eight rounds of .30 caliber ammunition, an M-1 rifle clip and a polishing rag. He was sitting alone on a palm log polishing the cartridges over and over, looking at them in an unfocused manner and smiling to himself.

Sometimes our country asks more of its men than they have to give.

Burnt Out

THE LONGER WE lived out of contact with the rest of the world, the longer we went without adequate nutrition and water and the more we were called upon to engage in repeated combat operations, the closer we came to getting what we called "burnt out," or less frequently, "the two thousand yard stare."

Burnt out was a hell of a state to be in. There was a pervasive uncaringness about almost anything. It permeated every tiniest corner of one's being. Nothing mattered. There was no particular sadness, neither was there joy. We probably would not have been able to sleep well had we had the luxury of a full night of uninterrupted calm without some kind of attack or the threat of one. These attacks, or possible attacks, required one to be aroused instantly with all one's faculties at maximum alert. My estimate is that this sort of thing came close to preventing long duration, deep, restorative sleep. One became pervasively exhausted and unable to maintain concentration and focus of attention. Irritability affected one's quality of judgement, even in simple matters. The two thousand yard stare had the additional aspect of one's tending to sit and stare uncomprehendingly into the distance. You didn't look at anything, you just stared.

There is now a medical name for this syndrome; further there is an acronym; still further, there is, I suspect, a gene alleged to be its cause. In today's world one can go to the highest peak of academic medicine if one can describe a syndrome, name it, invent an acronym for it and blame a gene for it.

The whole matter isn't that complicated. It certainly isn't that dramatic. It is just being used up, exhausted, worn out. We were burnt out. One of the only things of significance to most of us—the unlucky ones didn't even have this—was our treat of two bottles of beer every seven days. Since no one had a calendar, and we worked all day every day, we seldom knew which day or even which week or month it was; one simply counted seven days since the last treat to get to the next one.

One of our people, by chance, had run into a hometown friend who was in a navy supply unit. He quietly added us to his weekly supply list. We would send our one Jeep with its little trailer down the road every seventh day, apparently a Friday. The driver was accompanied by an armed guard, rifle loaded. The return trip from the navy supply unit was a slow, carefully driven one. Most of the time, if we got our full ration, which wasn't certain, we had to make two trips, fully loaded each trip.

Beer day, on the occasion I am going to tell you about, culminated in the late afternoon. Cases of beer were stacked where all could see and participate in the opening of each and the passing out to everyone of his two bottles.

The beer was one of the nastiest things I have ever tasted. It was semi-gelatinous, "ropey" beer— something I had never even heard of. The ropeyness results from the growth of contaminant microorganisms which produce a mucoid, nasty-tasting substance in the formerly liquid brew. The ropey beer was so viscid that it could not be poured easily from the bottle. If the bottle was turned upside down and struck on its base with your hand, you could then cause part of the contents to be forced out in a quivering glop. This usually splattered, much like ketchup would, were it treated similarly. This nasty stuff came to us under the euphemistic trade name of "Golden Glow." The nearest I can come in describing it to you is that it was an alcoholic, pale, yellowish-colored slime, most nearly resembling fermented snot.

We tried not to think of this as we sat down with a twig, gently pushed it down the neck of the bottle and even more gently withdrew it, with its adherent blob of alcoholic mucus. It was as nasty it sounds.

We were thankful for it.

As we sat around on palm logs, each with our twig and our two bottles, there was the sound of an aircraft engine at full throttle on the runway of the naval airfield atop the one hundred foot tall cliff behind our camp. Taking off over us at about one hundred ten or one hundred twenty foot altitude was what I can partly remember as something possibly called an F2M. This was a copy, it appeared, of a Grumman F6F, the Navy's most commonly used fighter aircraft. As best I could find out, which may not be correct, these things were made by General Motors. Whoever made them, suffice it to say that they were not highly regarded.

This one lived up to its reputation. As it strained to gain altitude directly above us, its engine suddenly quit dead, with not even a cough. It began to stall, but its momentum carried it just past us. It slammed into the ground at a sharp angle. The radial engine tore lose from the fuselage and went bounding along amongst the palm trees, finally coming to rest, smoking, at the edge of the beach, not far from our parked LVTs. The pilot bailed out, apparently pulling the rip cord of his chute as he leaped from the cockpit. This was his only hope of survival and was a clever, though desperate, maneuver. It was not enough. His chute caught the air and snapped partly open with a loud pop as a section of it filled suddenly. It opened before the pilot could clear the empenage of the F2M. His head hit the rudder post with a wet, dull thud, obviously killing him in an instant. His chute, not fully filled, carried his limp body down into the water just off our beach. People passing in a jeep on the dirt road between us and the beach saw the engine come past them like a giant, one-hundred-mile-an-hour smoking bowling ball. To say the least, their attention was caught. They ran to the dead pilot in the shallow water covering the reef.

None of our people even stirred from the palm logs on which we sat. There was no comment. We kept on working with our twigs, sucking the Golden Glow off them.

We were burnt out.

Volunteerism

WILSON WAS MY friend—an unlikely one for an Episcopal, Scottish, protected, sweet, Southern boy whose mother had taught him to be kind and attentive to ladies. Wilson had been orphaned at an early age by the deaths of both his Irish parents. He had been reared in East Orange, New Jersey, by an aunt whose constant economic struggle for survival left her little time or energy for anything else, especially Wilson.

He had managed to get into college with a football scholarship. He made enough to live on by playing professional football, concurrently, under a different name. He made extra money during vacation times by working as a sparring and training partner for "Two Ton" Tony Galento, the boxer. After one look, even the most fight-hungry marines would leave him alone.

He knew more about surviving in grim circumstances than anyone I have ever known. He tried to teach me some of this. I was, and am, deeply grateful. He told me once, "Sciple, you dumb son of a bitch, don't ever volunteer for anything. Make the bastards order you to do it if they want it done." I should have listened.

We took heavy losses in the assault on Guam. The Japs

had a well-organized beach defense and shot up our LVTs badly. I came in directly behind Wilson. His LVT had a turret which mounted a 37mm cannon; mine was open and had no turret.

Wilson refused to lock the top hatch on his turret, stating flatly that he would tear the head off any Nip who tried to open it and drop in a grenade. This idiosyncrasy probably saved his life. As Wilson's driver clawed his tracks into the soft beach sand at Agat, he hit a one-tit beach mine with the left track. The eleven pounds of picric acid explosive blew off the track and breached the hull of the amphibian tank. The blast came upward and blew Wilson completely out of the turret, through the hatch, and several feet up into the air above the turret. He fell headfirst onto the sand, knocking him into a punch-drunk state. He was staggering about trying to tackle the sand thrown up by the bursts of incoming mortar shells. It took four of us to hold him down.

Needless to say, Wilson was out of the fight for a few days, and I did not have his wisdom to rely on.

Major Drakeley had a mission to deliver several communications men and their ton or so of bulky gear to the south tip of the island. Guam is a large island; we, at Agat, were a long, long way from the south end. Even a momentary appraisal would reveal that there were many obvious and major problems in trying to carry out this mission. Among these were uncertainty as to whether the Japanese had withdrawn their troops from the area after they were sure our marines were committed fully to the landing halfway up the island at Agat and north of Agat at Agana. Our intelligence indicated that they had withdrawn, but you know how that is. Another problem was fuel: could we carry enough to get there and back? Yet another was maps: we had none. We had only a hand-drawn sketch made by a Chamorro man from that area who had made his way into our lines.

With all these uncertainties, Major Drakeley asked for an officer to volunteer. I did. I was given the mission, two of the best of the battered LVTs that we still had in running shape, and the right to ask for volunteer drivers and machine gunners for the .50 caliber and .30 caliber weapons we mounted.

We estimated our fuel consumption as best we could, given the many, only partly-known, variables. It was clear that there was little margin on fuel. We would have to conserve every drop and hope for favorable wind and sea conditions. There seemed no way to get adequate, up-to-date maps. We had to calculate our load by rough guess since we had no weighing device. We would have to carry adequate water and only K-rations for food in order to save weight.

It was certain that we could not make an overland journey. The Japs were still resisting strongly between our position at Agat and the south end where we had to go. The roads had been mined and those mines were just partly cleared. Our only reasonable course was to take our two LVTs out into the open sea and proceed a long, long way past sheer rock cliffs to a small bay where there was a beach, a small village, and a road which led up cliffs to another road which, in turn, led to the south tip. Our hand-drawn map showed these features.

We went by sea, arriving at the village quite late in the afternoon. We were fortunate that the tide and wind conditions were such that our six-inch freeboard kept out most of the water. As we crawled out of the ocean and up onto the beach, we came alongside a solidly-constructed stone monument with a bronze plaque. The plaque had an inscription in English. It commemorated the landing there of Magellan five hundred years earlier during his circumnavigation of the earth.

As I looked up at the cliffs behind the little village, I was appalled to see the "road" to the top. It was dirt, cut into the soft, rotted coral rock. Its angle of ascent must have been between thirty and forty degrees from the horizontal. Our LVTs surely, loaded heavily, did not have the power to climb this steep, steep grade. There was no other road. Cliffs surrounded the village. We could not proceed further south by sea since there was no beach or shoal south of our location where we could crawl up out of the water. My responsibility for my men began to weigh heavily on me.

Dusk was almost upon us. Night comes swiftly in the tropics after the sun sets. It was certain that we would have to spend the night where we then were. The wonderful, friendly Chamorro people had come down to welcome us. They told us there were no Japs in the immediate area. They offered us the schoolhouse for lodging. It was a small, wooden, white-painted building with four walls, a roof, a floor and nothing else. We were exhausted, our clothes wet for hours with salt water, facing a night on the floor and trying to sleep. The mosquitoes were terrible. We were finally bitten so massively that some of us were feverish.

I made a serious tactical error. In the face only of assurances from the local people that there were no enemy about, I put all of the men in the school building in order to try to get some rest. One blast of automatic weapons fire would have killed us. With the luck of a fool, we had no attack all night.

We got started not long after sunrise. Our map had its accuracy confirmed by the villagers. We had to ascend the great grade, perhaps four hundred to six hundred feet to the top, then continue south along a one-lane asphalt military road. This road had been built by U.S. forces many years before the Japanese attacked us at Pearl Harbor. First, though, we had to climb that thirty-to forty-degree grade to be able to get to the top.

We started our seven-cylinder, air-cooled, radial engines. We would need every bit of their original rated 250 horsepower. The engines and their oil needed to be fully warmed up. With a roar, the first LVT started up the grade. It got less than halfway up before it stalled. The driver, quite skillfully, managed to creep down by holding the LVT by its steering brakes. We were lucky we had not had a cata-strophic rollover.

I saw our only chance. My LVT had a slightly less worn engine and, hopefully, a stronger clutch than the one which had stalled. We unloaded it. I told our driver I didn't want him to get killed trying the climb, so I would try to get it to the top. I got the engine turning to its automatic-limit-ed maximum and engaged the clutch. I got no more than two-thirds of the way to the top when my engine rpms dropped below the critical limit. Just before the engine quit, I disengaged the clutch and held the LVT with its steering brakes.

Fortunately, my timing was correct to the second. The engine did not completely stall. After a few irregular, semi-stalling power strokes, my rpms began to rise toward the 2250 governor limit. I let in the clutch again, at the same time releasing my steering brakes. Again and again, with great good fortune, my timing was correct to the fraction of a second. I covered most of the remaining way to the top. I knew that I had a dry-sump engine with positive oil pickup so that the engine would not starve itself of lubrication on the extreme grade.

Would the clutch hold for two more burning-out tries? I was by now so far up the grade that I could not have backed down. I couldn't jump out. The steering brakes had to be held by hand. I had worked myself into a bad spot indeed. Two more tries, and I made it to the top with the engine overheated and the clutch smoking and close to burning. I kept the engine running to try to cool things down.

There was little question that the other LVT couldn't make it up. Our only course was to hand-carry the great load of equipment up the grade and reload it into my LVT. We dismounted the .50 caliber and .30 caliber machine guns and double-mounted them on my LVT. In addition, we removed an ignition part from the LVT still at the bottom of the grade so it could not be started except by us. All of us were sweat-soaked and exhausted.

The wind sweeping over us at our several-hundred-foot elevation began to cool us. We sat on the now-reloaded LVT, ate a K-ration and drank some of our water. After a bit of rest, we started south on the one-lane asphalt road. I was deeply thankful for that asphalt. As long as we could keep our tracks on it and saw no breaks in its surface, we could hope to avoid hitting a mine and killing us all. Though we had to keep alert, things went smoothly for a while. We all began to be able to glance about at the beautiful tropical growth to the east side of the road, the side away from the sea and several-hundred-foot-high cliffs.

Up ahead we saw a daunting obstacle. There was an exceptionally narrow but quite deep gorge in the soft rock. A stream had cut this and emptied into the sea at its end. The cliffs were precipitous. I climbed down them to try to find a way we could get the LVT down one side, into the water and up the other side. There was no way this could be done.

A tiny, narrow, concrete bridge spanned the 150-foot-wide chasm, four or five-hundred feet above the stream. Our LVT, unloaded, weighed in excess of 30,000 pounds. Its tracks were too wide for the road surface of the bridge. The only possible way to get the LVT across the chasm was to drive it up onto the railings on the side of the bridge. These were almost exactly as wide as the steel LVT tracks. We could only guess at the weight-bearing capacity of the bridge, but we were stopped unless we could get across it.

Perhaps one of the most courageous things I have ever done was to get our men out of the LVT and then drive it up onto the bridge railings. With Will Ault directing me, I drove the LVT over the bridge on the rails. I was shaking like a leaf when I got to the other side. We reloaded the LVT and started out for the south end.

We got there, unloaded the communications men and their equipment and left. I drove back across the tiny bridge on its railings. I trembled this time too. When we arrived at the great incline above the Magellanic village, I got the men out of the LVT, put it in lowest gear and started to creep down the grade. Even in first gear and fully off the throttle, my engine rpms began to rise. If I went over the limited 2250, the engine might disintegrate. I held onto the steering brakes and hoped my way down.

We got down without a wreck, remounted the .50 caliber and .30 caliber machine guns on the other LVT and replaced its ignition part. We started it, said goodbye to the villagers and crawled down the beach into the water. After running about half of the way back to Agat, conditions changed. We had to slow. My LVT began to run low on fuel. We shut it down after tying it to the other one. My men and I got into the other LVT, no mean feat to accomplish in the open sea without an injury.

We proceeded at an agonizingly slow pace and threw up a column of white water behind us. This column apparently was sighted by a small patrol vessel which came roaring toward us with her forward 20mm cannon at the ready. The skipper was about to fire when he recognized the LVT and our helmets. He raised hell with us. We kept on paddling along.

Just as the towing LVT began to run low on fuel, we saw our beach at Agat. My crew and I got back into our LVT, started the engine, threw off our tow line and started for shore. We arrived, both LVTs, on the beach with only a gallon or so of fuel left. I thanked our men for their fine work and felt a great burden of responsibility drop from my shoulders. We were back. We had not lost a man or even had an injury. We had accomplished our mission.

As I stood there, deeply thankful, a runner came up to me with the message that I was to report to headquarters immediately. I did this, expecting to have a commendation for my men and me. What I got was a royal chewing out and threat of a general court martial. I was stunned.

What had happened, apparently, was that Major Drakeley had failed to notify the navy that we were on a mission, the patrol vessel that spotted us had radioed in about us, and the navy brass chewed out our General. I was blamed.

Ah, Wilson lad, 'tis so hard to learn from thee.

Bacteriological Warfare

SOME OF THE principles of bacteriological warfare are direct and simple. Their results, when applied, can be profound. One principle is to use an agent to which your own people are immune or already exposed. Such an agent is far more effective if it is transmitted amongst the enemy widely and with great ease. Another is that the most valuable agents are those that cause protracted, severe, disabling illness, but which usually do not kill. Even in cultures where human life is not highly valued, a trained fighter is important enough to use scarce resources in trying to salvage him or her. A long-sick fighter can be a far greater loss to an enemy than a rapidly killed one.

The more you know about the agent you are using and the less the enemy knows about it, the better it can serve your purposes. As a corollary to this principle, the more numerous are other agents which can cause somewhat similar signs of illness, the better your agent may be in confusing the enemy's attempts at countermeasures, thereby causing great losses.

The best agent is the one you have available. It is better if it is cheap. It is better yet if it can be spread easily and without detection.

The Japanese brought together all these principles on the men of the Lost Company. Our sick men were so numerous that we were, for a time, unable to perform our missions.

The source of drinking water in our temporary camp at Guam was a well. This well had been dug many years before our arrival by the native Chamorro people and was known to the Japs. It was about fifteen feet deep and supplied cool water. Our men drank it in quantity in the tropical heat and were thankful to have it.

The Japs used picric acid as an explosive in many of their munitions. Though we in the Lost Company knew nothing of the concerns of naval medical personnel about leaching of picric acid from unexploded shells into the groundwater, it was something that doctors treating illnesses in our men had to keep in mind as a possible cause of those illnesses.

Japanese physicians had long and wide experience with infectious hepatitis. They knew that infection with some strains of virus could be passed in contaminated water. Our doctors knew little of infectious hepatitis. They clearly did not know what was going on with us.

Further, and confusingly, we had earlier been placed on atabrine as a prophylaxis for malaria while we were at Guadalcanal. Atabrine was an anti-malarial drug developed by the Germans when their supply of quinine, the then standard anti-malarial drug, was cut off. When the Japs cut off the U.S. supply, we started using atabrine. It was a yellow dye and tasted, at best, terrible. Our people would take the tablets at the daily dispensing, put them in their mouths, carry them away unswallowed, and later spit them out on the ground. Not only that, on our awful 68-day voyage from Tulagi in the Solomon Islands to the Marianas Islands, we ran short of everything, atabrine included. As a result, by the time we got to Guam, few of our Lost Company men had had any appreciable amount of atabrine in many weeks. I tell you all this so that you will understand the ridiculousness of the diagnosis for the approximately one-half of our men who came down in about a week with febrile illness where their skin was colored yellow. That navy doctor's diagnosis was "atabrine poisoning." As good as any, I guess, if you don't have the faintest notion of what the hell you are dealing with.

The illness that almost all of us in the Lost Company eventually developed was a debilitating one. We had fever for a few days with marked loss of appetite, right upper abdominal pain, loose stools and a yellow tint (jaundice) to our eyes and skin. Our urine was dark yellow in color. This went on for many days. Recovery was slow, with weakness and exhaustion lasting for months. I was sick for more than six months, with persisting jaundice, daily vomiting episodes, extreme physical weakness and loss of about one-third of my body weight.

What probably happened in our Lost Company episode may turn out to be one of the most efficient applications of bacteriological warfare ever devised. I doubt strongly that we had picric acid poisoning. In the first place, there weren't that many unexploded Japanese shells in our camp area. In addition, rainwater leaching of picric acid from a ruptured bomb or shell would take considerable time. Further time would be needed for rainwater containing leached out picric acid to seep through a number of feet of soil to enter the groundwater in any appreciable concentration.

The Japs often tried to slip into our camp in the middle of the night. We caught several of them doing this. I thought they were trying to steal food or weapons, and they may well have been, amongst other activities. My thinking changed when we caught one with his pants down. He was at our well. He had passed a loose stool into it. It was his last one, ever. I believe the Jap commanders ordered their sick men to foul our well repeatedly. They were undetected for a long time.

Many Japanese were carriers of the infectious hepatitis virus. I believe that with great creativity and cleverness, their commanders used a weapon against us that cost them nothing. It cost us a great deal. It almost cost me my life.

What an immensely high benefits/cost ratio for them: bacteriological warfare at its best.

The Admiral

I HAVE TOLD you earlier how we lost many fine marines in our assault on Guam. The Japanese had built a perimeter defense just behind the beaches at the village of Agat. In addition, they had a mobile force in the interior of Guam, a good-sized island. This mobile force was composed partly of Imperial Marines; these men were six feet or so tall and fierce fighters, to whom death in the emperor's service was an honor and an assured entrance into heaven. I enjoyed honoring them.

After our successful, but bloody, assault and occupation of part of the island, we were ordered to move our battered landing vehicles several miles north to an unmined beach, where we could attempt to make repairs and get as many as possible ready for future combat.

Our men were mourning their lost comrades. We had few spare parts to work with. We had almost no replacement clothing. Our food was so short that our men pooled their money and bought for slaughter a carabao, a large Asian water buffalo. We existed, in part, by begging from the members of a nearby battalion of Seabees, whose kindnesses I will never forget. We were trying to get ready for the next operation, almost surely another bloody one.

In the midst of this mess and in the middle of the night, a group of Imperial Marines slipped into our camp and began firing. I awakened to see a muzzle flash from a rifle pointed in my direction. I rolled off my partly rotted canvas cot and pulled out the .45 caliber pistol that I wore day and night in a stinking shoulder holster. The first instant after a muzzle flash at night, you know exactly where it came from. The second instant you know approximately. The third instant you have no idea.

For this reason, I did not fire. I lay on the night-wet soil and waited. By this time there was more firing. The Imperial Marines were implacable. We drove the bastards to our south and out of our camp. By this time, it was almost daylight. As our few tents gradually became visible, they looked like Swiss cheese. A quick check revealed that we had no dead, for which we were deeply thankful. The few wounds were minor ones. We had made it through another night. We continued to drive the Nips south.

Our captain scrounged up a flame-thrower from somewhere. He and the two flame-thrower men followed our people as they drove the Imperial Marines to the south. After a short time, the Japs ceased firing and seemed to disappear. Our people were baffled until they broke out of the heavy vegetation and saw a coral-rock cliff ahead of them. The soft rock face was penetrated by a tunnel opening about eighty to one hundred feet above the plain where our men stood. The Japanese had dug what must have been a considerable-sized cave. There was a large, fanned-out pile of spoil rock where they had brought the dug rock from the tunnel to its mouth and dumped it down the cliff.

Those of you who know mining or have seen shafts dug horizontally into a cliff face are familiar with the half-cone which the dumped rock forms. The larger pieces of rock roll farther down the slope and form a wide, semicircular base. The smaller pieces and finely-ground powder form a tip to the conical shape. The tip is at the mouth of the shaft. As you can imagine, climbing this spoil is difficult at best and near impossible to do without leaving tracks.

Our men saw fresh tracks leading into the mouth of the cave. Almost surely, the Imperial Marines, our guests of the just-ended night, had holed up in it. As we started to climb the spoil pile, the Nips appeared near the opening and started throwing grenades. These rolled down the steep slope, but took so much time bouncing amongst the soft coral rock boulders that they detonated before reaching our people. We poured rifle fire into the cave mouth, but we soon came to see in the increasingly bright daylight that there was a sharp right-angle bend in the shaft not far behind its opening in the cliff. The Nips retired back into the tunnel and into what we later discovered was a large, dug-out room. We were, clearly, at an impasse.

With great courage, our captain and the two flame-thrower operators started climbing the spoil pile. This was agonizingly slow and difficult. They were drenched with sweat and close to exhaustion by the time they reached the tunnel mouth, some fifteen to twenty feet below the top of the near-vertical cliff. They stood in the mouth and saw the right angle turn in the shaft. Knowing that the flame-thrower fluid would not squirt past the ninety-degree turn, they went down the shaft the few feet to the turn. At the turn, they put the nozzle around the corner and began to squirt without igniting the fluid. They hoped to get in enough fluid to be able, at best, to burn the Japanese alive, or at worst, to use up the oxygen so they would suffocate. For us, this meant that all three men would have to back out of the tunnel and get away from the mouth before pulling the igniter on the nozzle and setting off the hoped-for incineration.

There were several problems with this plan. The first was how far back in the tunnel the Imperial Marines were and how might their expected response be countered. The second was whether there was an air vent from the room at the end of the tunnel to the level ground at the top of the cliff, perhaps a distance of twenty feet. A third problem was how to back out of the tunnel while carrying the flame-thrower supply tanks. It is far easier to go into a shaft with these strapped to you than it is to back out of one.

The fourth problem was an entirely unanticipated one. In loading the flame-thrower, the fire-intensifying powder should be dissolved in diesel fuel. Someone had gotten hold of a 55-gallon drum that obviously contained petroleum distillate. The problem, then unknown to the captain, was that the distillate was not diesel fuel but high octane aviation gasoline. When our men had the squirting almost completed and were ready to start backing out of the tunnel, one of the Imperial Marines threw a grenade. It detonated before it got to the right angle near the mouth of the cave where our men were. Not a one of the metal fragments hit our people, but the flash set off the high octane gas vapor. Our captain and the two flame-thrower men were blown out of the mouth of the cave in a great flash. They came rolling down the rock spoil with their clothes and hair on fire. Strangely, the fire in the tunnel went out with the blast. The Japanese survived in the room at the end of the tunnel and continued to throw out grenades until their supply was exhausted.

I was our captain's executive officer, now in command with the burned men being carried off to the nearest medical aid station. I was faced with some rather difficult choices. Should I let the Nips be, to come out at dark and attack us again? For a number of reasons, this did not seem wise. Should I try to resurrect the flame-thrower, reload it with fluid and try again? The flame-thrower was battered beyond repair, and the two operators were badly burned. Should I try something else?

There is, or was, a famous Marine Corps admonition: "Do something, even if it's wrong." Remembering this and that our Seabee friends had some boxes of explosive they had been using to blow stumps, I sent two of our men to try to beg some. It turned out that all the Seebees had left, or all they could spare us, was 60% dynamite. In that day, dynamite was wax-paper-wrapped sticks of sawdust soaked with nitroglycerine. Forty percent was fairly dry and a little more stable in the tropical heat. Fifty percent was problematic. Sixty percent was exceedingly dangerous and was used only in special circumstances. I suspect that was why the Seabees still had it and were willing to let our people beg it from them. Not only was the 60% particularly unstable, there was such a high proportion of nitroglycerine that the sawdust often could not absorb all of it. The oily nitroglycerine would ooze out of the sawdust and out of the brown wax paper onto the wooden boxes in which it was packed.

Nitroglycerine has potent physiologic action in the human body. Among other things, it relaxes the muscle fibers in arteries. The arteries have less tension and the blood from the heart travels through them in greater amounts and with a great, hammering pulse. Nitroglycerine is absorbed through intact skin. When one has it in quantity on one's skin, one can get a catastrophic "dynamite headache," where there is some question as to whether it is relaxing the arteries in one's head or blowing up inside it.

The wooden boxes were wet with leaked nitroglycerine. The Seabees had given us three one-hundred-pound cases. I had a strong and courageous man with me named Red Atkins. He and I each shouldered a one-hundred-pound case. We had another man who took the third case in a Jeep along

a dirt road that led to the top of the cliff where we had discovered a near-vertical air shaft opening that ventilated the
underground room in which we believed the Japanese marines were. Our Jeep driver moved off with the most delicate easing of the clutch that one can imagine. He, like Red
and I, knew that the 60% dynamite in the tropical heat was
exceedingly unstable. To make it worse, he carried blasting
caps and a coil of Primacord with him in the front seat. Primacord is a type of knit-covered, corded TNT. When detonated at one end, the explosion travels almost instantly to
the other end, exploding all the way.

Our plan was for Red and me to climb the spoil pile,
each carrying a one-hundred-pound case. I carried electric
blasting caps and a coil of wire to string back down the slope
to a distant point where one of our people guarded a dou-
ble-handled magneto or "shooter" box. We figured, Red and
I, that our approximately eighty-foot climb would be pain-
fully slow and give time for our man to drive over the mile
or so road to the top of the cliff. There he would position his
case over the air shaft, press some caps into the pasty dynamite after peeling back the brown paper wrapper, and gently press in some Primacord alongside the detonators. He
then would string the Primacord along the ground to the
edge of the cliff and drop the rest of the cord down to Red
and me, while holding his end firmly so it would not pull
out of the case over the air shaft. Surprisingly, this necessi-
ty-rigged arrangement worked. About the time Red and I

got to the mouth of the cave, our man dropped the remaining Primacord over the cliff and it came close enough to Red for him to catch it. There was a long enough piece for him, and then for me, to press it into the pliable dynamite. I then pressed in the blasting caps I had brought up with me, attached the lead wire to the caps and started down the slope. Red and I slowly made our way down while I paid out the lead wire carefully so it would not pull the caps out of the dynamite and away from the Primacord. We slipped, slid, scratched and cut ourselves trying to get back down. We were sweat-soaked and plastered with orange-colored coral dirt. I was so scared that I had wet my pants when a Jap grenade had detonated in the tunnel around the right-angle turn. For whatever reason, our charge did not go up. Perhaps the soft, rotted coral rock absorbed the energy of the grenade. My headache was awful. I had vomited from extreme exhaustion.

Red and I were hardly candidates for admission to an ambassador's drawing room. We had bloody hands and faces from our cuts and scratches; we were soaked with sweat and orange-colored from plastered coral dust. Our man with the magneto, or "shooter" box, looked Red and me over. He said to me, "You want me to shoot it, Lieutenant?" I said, "Hell, no, let a man who carried it up shoot it," and turned to Red. Red looked at me saying, "I'm too tired to give a damn, you shoot it." I made sure our man at the top of the cliff was out of range, connected the lead wires to the box, yelled "fire in the hole" as loudly as I could, and pushed down the handle.

As luck would have it, and by a chance in hundreds or thousands, our length of strung Primacord was almost exactly the length necessary to give a double explosion, with one following the other by perhaps a hundredth of a second. The detonations appeared to reinforce one another through a shock wave carried through the main tunnel and the vertical air shaft.

There was an immense, rumbling blast. A Buick Roadmaster-sized piece of coral rock, trailing a pandanus tree and other vegetation, rose hundreds of feet into the air and fell with a thump uncomfortably close to us. A great cloud of brown dynamite smoke and orange-colored coral rock powder drifted down over the whole area.

As the smoke and dust cloud began to clear, a navy lieutenant commander in a starched khaki uniform and shined oxford shoes came running up. He looked about imperiously and demanded, "Who is in charge here?"

I walked up to him and said, "I am, Commander."

He said, "I am the admiral's aide. The admiral wants to see you at once." This was so bizarre and out of context with the grim circumstances that I thought it must be some kind of joke. One must understand that there are few creatures more precious and piss-antish than an admiral's aide.

This one led the league in both aspects. I came close to laughing in his face.

In his most officious manner, he ordered me to follow him. I did. We soon came to, of all things, a gray-painted, open command car. In it was a Vice Admiral, three Navy nurses and a large picnic basket. A great lump of blasted-off coral lay nearby. The Admiral looked at me and said, "What do you think you're doing, Lieutenant?"

I paused to gather enough strength to reply, looked him straight in the eyes and said, "I'm killing people, Admiral."

There was a silence, he looked a bit odd and one of the nurses laughed nervously. Not another word was said. He motioned to his driver to go. They left.

Reconnaissance
Marshall Islands: The Unknown

THIS STORY HAS to do with matters for some of which there may be no other written record. It is out of temporal sequence due to its length. It involves a number of related events which occurred as parts of a protracted and dangerous reconnaissance into unknown enemy territory.

It is about our company operations in the early part of the United States naval thrust across the Central Pacific, undertaken after our nation began to recover from grievous losses early in WW II, subsequent to the sneak attack by the Japanese on Pearl Harbor. It may not be written about elsewhere because our company was abandoned at Kwajalein Atoll after our attack on the atoll and its capture. We were left on the few acres of a tiny islet several miles down the reef from the islands of Roi and Namur. We were ordered to occupy this wee bit of coral sand, though we had no water, food, ammunition, fuel, oil, spare parts, tools, clothing, shelter or medical care. We had no sources of getting any of these. Just to live from day to day we had to scavenge, beg and steal.

We were on no personnel roster. We were on no pay schedule and received no pay for a period of many months.

In that day our only communication was by mail. We had no mail at all for six months. There was no communication with the outside world for that entire time except that we had orders following other orders for repeated combat operations. We were able to maintain our LVTs in running shape only by our men's wonderful inventiveness and capacity to scavenge spare parts. From an administrative standpoint, we failed to exist.

I tell you all this again and again so that you may be able, in your own experience, to feel a bit of how awful it was for our men. For them to be able to operate in multiple combat situations in a consistently superior manner was phenomenal. Their willingness and their ability to do so was quietly heroic. That heroism has never been recognized.

I ask you to recognize it now.

In the political settlement after the first World War, the Japanese got the Marshall Islands in the Central Pacific Ocean. Whether or not the political settlement intended it, or even allowed it, the Japs assumed complete control, even to the point of denying entrance into the eastern chain of the Marshalls, facing toward the far distant Hawaiian Islands. The western chain faces toward Guam, the Philippines, Indonesia and Asia. It, too, was closed off from outside contact.

We in the United States had little or no knowledge of what was going on in the Marshalls but became progressively more concerned when rumors circulated that the Japs were building extensive military facilities there including, but not limited to, airfields, communication centers, coastal defense emplacements, and naval bases. Our people believed that the most formidable of these fortifications were in the eastern chain, but we really did not have much solid information. This lack of information was particularly true of the western chain of islands, among which were Kwajalein, Bikini, Namu, Namorik, Ailinglapalap and Ebon Atolls. Kili Island, a non-atoll single island, was also in this group.

The Japanese had many victories early in World War II: their sneak attack on Pearl Harbor, the assault on Wake Island, taking the Philippines and the Dutch East Indies; New Guinea; the Solomon Islands; Burma and East Asia. They came terrifyingly close to defeating us.

As we began to recover from the terrible losses, our navy gradually grew stronger in the Pacific, enough to support a northern move through the Aleutians, a southern advance through the Solomons and New Guinea and then a main thrust across the Central Pacific toward Japan. Much of the fighting in this central thrust was by U.S. Marines. It started in the Marshall Islands. Our amphibian tractor company was part of this fight.

With our minimal knowledge of the extent of the Japanese fortification during the twenty years of their possessing the Marshalls, it seemed wisest to try to bypass the eastern islands and attack the military center at Kwajalein in the western chain. Kwajalein Atoll is a large one. It has been said to resemble a giant string of pearls lying on the surface of the sea. The string is the coral reef and the pearls are the small islands. If one makes this comparison, it is essential to understand that there is a hell of a lot of string and very few pearls. The reef is often barely covered or barely uncovered by sea water at lowest tide. High tide is only a few feet above this. The coral sand islands, in turn, are only a few inches to a few feet in elevation above high tide. The elongated, more or less circular reef at Kwajalein encloses a lagoon with relatively shallow water. There are passes in the reef where there is enough water to allow transit of large, deep draft warships and cargo vessels. Outside the reef there is a precipitous drop toward abyssal depths, many thousands of feet.

Our assault on the joined islands of Roi and Namur at Kwajalein Atoll was successful after a few days, but costly. The Japanese defended tenaciously; we took almost no prisoners. We had many killed and wounded. Our landing vehicles were able to enter the lagoon, claw their way up over the reef and land our marines on the lagoon sides of the two islands. We had many wrecked LVTs.

After the fighting and capture of Roi and Namur, our support vessels began to load the marine division troops and our other three companies of LVTs for a return to a base in the far distant Hawaiian Islands for replacement of casualties, resupply, the repair of LVTs and replacement of other equipment.

Our company had no orders to leave. The ships sailed away without us. Two years passed before we saw our comrades again. Whatever the administrative confusion, we were in a grim position. We were a Lost Company. That was apparent to all hands as we watched our people sail away.

Finally, weeks later, we did get orders. Those orders were not to return to the Hawaiian Islands but to carry out a reconnaissance through the western chain of the Marshalls, a vast and little-known area. No one had any idea what we would encounter.

Our combat force included parts of the 22nd Marine Regiment, two or three Landing Ships, Tank (LSTs), a large fleet mine sweeper, a Fletcher class destroyer, a Bristol class destroyer and a small, open-deck, tank-carrying vessel. The Fletcher class destroyer was the Black #666. I remember her well, since I was nearly killed in Ailinglapalap lagoon by ricochets from her five-inch guns. A naval officer was the commander of our ships and troops.

The force I have described was even more cobbled together than it sounds. Our LVT company people had never worked with the 22nd Marine Regiment people who did not know or trust us, because they had not been in combat with us.

I had never even seen our two main warships, the destroyers. Our LSTs, onto which we were to load, were unknown to us as well. We had never heard the name of the naval officer commanding our combined forces.

If you would like to cook up a disaster, the above is a sure recipe for it. To be effective and to avoid catastrophic foul-ups, everyone in a landing force has to work together, smoothly. The actions of any part of it must be coordinated with the actions of the others. Our landings were complex operations even under the best of conditions.

Our marines climbed into their assigned LVTs while we were still loaded inside the long, enclosed tank deck of the LST. The ship's beam was so narrow that the tank deck could barely, just barely, accommodate two LVTs side-by-side. The approximately twelve inches between the two was about equal to the distance from the other side of each LVT and the steel hull of the ship. We were packed like sardines in a floating can, two, side-by-side, jammed together rows. We had no equipment to lash each tracked vehicle to the deck or hull of the ship. This meant, of course, that the 33,000-pound, steel-tracked LVTs could slide back and forth on the smooth steel deck when the ship began to roll in a heavy sea, though there was only about a foot between each side-by-side LVT and only about a foot between each LVT and the hull of the ship. When the ship rolled heavily, there was sliding of the LVTs with jamming between each other and the ship's hull, leaving a nearly three-foot gap on the other side. As the ship rolled to that other side, as it was certain to do, there would be a terrible hammering blow to the hull.

To those few of you, surely a very few indeed, who have

survived a shifting cargo in a ship in a heavy sea, I offer my deepest respect. We well might not have survived ours had we had a storm. With the luck of the draw, we had calm seas. I was exceedingly thankful; we would never have made it through even a moderately rough sea. We had no reason to believe that our commander had any experience in assault landing operations using LVTs. Few naval officers did at that time. Further, the knowledge of such commanders was woefully deficient in what we LVT people could, as well as could not, do.

Our orders were at times absurdly out of sync with the existing realities. The same kind of inexperience in naval officers was seen in ordering naval gunfire to support our landings. They may have been taught in midshipman's school about battleship broadsides or cruiser anti-aircraft fire, but they often knew so little about ship-to-shore pre-landing suppression of enemy fire as to be dangerous to our own forces. Ship-to-shore fire in support of advancing or pinned down friendly troops is still more demanding of experience, skill and judgment.

Our lack of an accompanying hospital ship gave us all a sinking feeling. Perhaps you can imagine yourself with a massive organ-tearing shrapnel wound to the abdomen with the nearest well-equipped surgical suite on a hospital ship several hundred miles away across submarine-infested waters. We were almost certain on a long reconnaissance of many defended atolls to have casualties. How could our wounded men be cared for adequately? We had no answer. The entire reconnaissance, before we even got underway from Kwajalein, left me with a deep sense of foreboding.

Our loaded force got underway, sailed forty miles or so down the lagoon and exited into the open sea via the pass next to Kwajalein Island. Our LST was the next to last ship in our force to clear the pass. Following us was a small, open-deck, tank-carrying vessel loaded with two Sherman tanks, the only armor we had.

As I watched, the small vessel began to encounter the great, heaving Pacific swells as she came through the pass in the reef. She simply could not take the seas with the load she was carrying and began to founder. There was no way to lower her ramp, put one tank in gear, drive it off into the 10,000-foot deep sea, and thus halve her burden. Had it been possible to drive off one tank without the sea rushing in through her open bow, she might have been able to continue with us and offer us at least a single tank for our soon to come combat. This was not possible, nor was it even attempted.

With fine seamanship and great good fortune, her crew managed to bring her about—just barely—without sinking. As dusk began to approach, I could see her return through the pass and into the calm waters of the lagoon. There went our tanks. We were on our own and headed for a series of unknowns. The first of these was Ailinglapalap.

Ailinglapalap Atoll

We had almost no intelligence to guide us. We did know that Ailinglapalap was the center of the civil administration of the western chain of the Marshalls. We knew further that F6F fighter aircraft had flown over the atoll several days before our arrival and that they had not been fired upon by any large caliber weapons. If they had taken reconnaissance photographs, we did not have these available to us to aid in the planning of our attack.

Knowing almost nothing, our small armada arrived off the atoll soon after first light. The large, fleet minesweeper prepared to enter a pass in the reef across the wide lagoon from the long, narrow, main island. We all held our breaths as the minesweeper slowly and carefully entered the pass. No mines were detonated; she passed into the lagoon untouched. She drew no fire from shore. There was a great sigh of relief on everyone's part, the loudest from the crew of the minesweeper, I suspect.

Our other ships entered the pass one by one and lay in the lagoon. We still drew no fire from shore. Were the Japs holding their fire until they had us cold or had they no major defenses? We set about answering this question.

The LSTs moved toward the middle of the perhaps one-to-two-mile-wide lagoon. They opened their bow doors, lowered their ramps, and our troop-loaded LVTs moved down the ramps into the calm waters of the lagoon. Our LVTs were organized into three waves. These waves were each composed of six vehicles. The waves formed up in lines parallel to the beach, the latter two waves following the first at about two hundred yard intervals.

I happened to be in the third wave, where I had an excellent view of what was going on both ahead of and behind us. I cannot remember any naval gunfire supporting our landing. I saw no enemy fire directed toward us. What I did see surprised me. Our larger destroyer, the Black, began moving from the lagoon, through the pass and out to sea. I had no idea why she was doing this. My quick mental search came up with a number of possibilities, none of them probable. We were approaching the narrow beach. I could see no shot-up or stranded LVTs ahead of us. There seemed to be no coral heads to impede us or tear open our hulls.

We landed our load of marines well up on the beach. They immediately disappeared into the palm trees and bushes. We had drawn no enemy fire that I knew of and were undamaged—a relief. After our marines left our vehicle, we started back across the lagoon to load mortar shells, small arms ammunition and fresh water. Our orders were to bring loads across the lagoon, over the beach and, if possible, up the island to our advancing troops.

It was far easier and safer to load the heavy ammunition with the LVTs back inside the vessel on its tank deck. We could not climb up the ramp nose-first with our LVTs because the tank deck was too narrow to allow us to turn our LVTs around so that we could leave the ship by going down her ramp nose-first. We had to enter the sea nose-first, since backing down the twenty-five-to-thirty degree angled ramp would swamp our vehicle. Its heavy, rear-mounted 250 hp radial engine and great clutch plates would sink it. We had lost more than one LVT proving this; we could not afford to lose another.

This meant we had to climb the steep ramp and enter the opened bow doors of the LST by backing out of the sea, onto the steep ramp, up the ramp, through the narrow bow doors of the ship and onto its tank deck. This would allow us to return to the sea bow-first without swamping the LVT.

Backing a 33,000-pound, seven-foot-wide, steel-tracked vehicle up a 25 degree-angled ramp required great skill and courage. Our drivers had both. We usually got onto the tank deck without injury to our men or to the LVT.

After returning from the beach to the ship, I was lying still in the water waiting for the LST to open her bow doors and lower her ramp so that our driver could back onto the tank deck and we could load the ammunition and supplies. We had a few minutes to rest while this was going on .

Then it happened. There was no more than a tenth of a second that I heard it coming. There was a tremendous explosion in the water just a few feet from us. Again, the luck of the draw—I wasn't hit by the shrapnel. Another shell landed between our LVT and the LST. A third shell, either hit her open deck or exploded near it. I heard later that it killed some marines and wounded others.

I had no idea what was happening, but guessed that the Japanese had finally opened up on us, hoping to sink our LSTs and thereby cut off ammunition and supplies from the troops ashore. It seemed a reasonable guess at the time. I acted on it instantly, ordering our driver to get as far from the ship as we could and as fast as we could. I couldn't help the ship, but I might be able to save us. My estimate was that the Japs would continue to fire at the ship, and we had a chance not to be hit by what I was sure was at least 155mm cannon fire. After a few more rounds, which landed in the water away from the LST, the firing ceased. The ship had been hit; we in our LVT had not.

My estimate had been wrong, but my response to my wrong estimate was right. When you are faced with the necessity of making a life and death decision with only a few observations to go on, the life-threatening situation may have a cause entirely different from that you have estimated to be the true one. This was the case in the lagoon at Ailinglapalap. What had happened, as best I was able to piece together later, was that the commander had ordered the Black out of the lagoon to offer fire support to the marines on shore. This was bizarre, since the time we most needed naval gunfire was before and during our landing, not afterward, and certainly not on the beach where we had not long before landed and where we were to bring in supplies.

As best I could find out, the Black was ordered to leave the lagoon before our initial landing on the beach. She came out of the pass into the open sea and proceeded in a partially circular path to arrive finally at a point off the sea side of the long, narrow island, almost exactly opposite to where we had already landed on the lagoon side beach. She then opened fire with her five-inch-38 main armament. Ailinglapalap Island rises so little above high tide that its elevation was actually less than the elevation of the Black's five turrets. She must have had to depress her guns to be able to hit the island. Hit it she did. At relatively point-blank range and with her five-inch-38 guns depressed beyond horizontal, the shells ricocheted off the sand without detonating. Not only was the Black opposite our landing beach, she was also opposite our ships in the lagoon and was firing toward them. The unexploded ricocheting shells landed and detonated in the water perilously close to my LVT and on or near our LST. This was an idiotic, green-to-combat screw-up. I heard that the commander was relieved of duty, precipitously.

Shaken but unharmed, we finally got our ammunition and supplies loaded and carried them in to the landing beach. So much time had passed that our marines had advanced far up the island with only slight resistance. I was in a position where I had a load of ammunition and supplies, presumably by now badly needed by our advancing troops; I knew they had no trucks in which to carry these supplies.

To unload our mortar shells and ammunition on the beach where they would then have to be hand-carried to the line of fighting seemed to me to be an abandonment of our responsibility to our comrades. At the same time, I knew that our thin-hulled LVTs wouldn't protect us against small arms fire, much less cannon fire. Further, our tracks would almost surely set off land mines should the Japs have planted them in our path. I knew that we did not have the power to knock down full-grown coconut palm trees, of which there were a great many. We could get stuck trying to force our way between them.

I was in a command position and had to make a decision. I decided to order our several loaded LVTs to remain on the beach while I went on foot to determine where we needed to go and how to get there. This was not a decision I was pleased with. I simply was the one best qualified to determine the matters that had to be determined. I was in a bad spot and frightened. I had to do what I had to do.

I took my wretched little .30 caliber carbine, not a lot better than nothing, and set out toward where I could hear sporadic rifle fire. After moving as carefully and quickly as I could while assessing our potential for moving LVTs through the area, I began to smell a stench so overpowering as to nauseate me. I soon came onto the source. A shell had hit and blasted open a large, wooden, Japanese box of canned fish heads. Many cans were ruptured. Foul-smelling fish heads in great numbers were spattered all over the vegetation. I had about a second to be amazed at how any human being, even a Jap, could eat anything like this. The stench followed me as I moved along. My estimate was that, with care, we could drive our steel-tracked vehicles through the area I had traversed, stinking or not.

I was reared during the Great Depression and had seldom even been out of the state of Georgia before I entered the Marine Corps. We had to go and live with my grandmother when my father's business was foreclosed on by his bankers. My grandmother didn't have mechanical refrigeration. She cooled her baked goods in a wooden cabinet which had two doors opening forward. The doors had wood frames with large galvanized metal sheets, set one in each frame. The metal sheets had complex floral patterns punched in them with a small, sharp nail. This allowed heat and moisture to escape while keeping houseflies out. The cabinet was called a pie safe.

With this kind of background, I believe you can understand my disorientation as I moved, stinking of foul fish heads, through the exquisite tropical island.

The disorientation I felt was nothing compared to the surreal experience I was about to have. As I moved on past the fish heads, I came toward a clearing. In the clearing sat an absolutely beautifully constructed *fale*, a thatched house built on posts with its floor several feet above ground level. The *fale* floor was so situated that the house looked out over a beach and the glistening sapphire sea beyond. I stood in amazement at this unexpected beauty; fortunately, I was not so taken by the scene as to abandon all caution. I stood still in the vegetation for a long time, observing and listening. I could hear our 22nd Regiment Marines on ahead of me; I had partly overtaken them. I had found an excellent spot to be able to bring our waiting LVTs and unload their ammunition and supplies. It was time for me to return to the LVTs and get them moving up.

With an uncharacteristic lack of caution, I moved toward the *fale*. I was out in the open, a prime target for anyone in the house who cared to kill me. Knowing all this, I kept going up onto the porch and looked in through the door. Foolhardily, I entered. To my immense relief, no Jap was there. The room was a kitchen. It, too, had no mechanical refrigeration. Along the wall opposite me, and in full daylight, sat a pie safe, a wood and metal cabinet just like the one in my grandmother's kitchen 7000 miles away. Even the nail-punched, floral pattern in the metal door sheets was identical to my grandmother's. I felt like I was in two different places at the same time. I went on back and got our LVTs up to the clearing and unloaded the ammunition and supplies.

How does one integrate this kind of happening into one's body of experience? It has been more than fifty years, and I have never been able to do it.

Namorick Atoll

Namorick was a small, two-island atoll, with a narrow pass into a small lagoon. We were to land with almost nothing in intelligence information about it, except its name. Our force had been divided; we had fewer than half of our ships, men and LVTs; again we were in a dangerous situation.

The pass was found to be too shallow to admit our ships. This meant that we had to drive our LVTs down the L ST's ramp while the ship rolled and pitched in offshore waters. The LST's captain was a skilled ship handler, as well as an intelligent and decent man. He positioned his ship so as to diminish the roll and pitch as much as possible. With his and his helmsman's skill, we got into the water without sinking even one of our LVTs. I did not have time to think of the far more difficult task of backing up the ramp when we had to re-enter the tank deck of the ship upon our return to it.

There wasn't time to think because I was immediately presented with another problem. We had to land our troops by driving our LVTs through large breaking waves onto a beach where there appeared to be little reef for us to get our tracks onto so that we could climb out of the water. I feared that there might be large coral heads just beneath the surface. We could overturn, strand or rip open our thin steel LVT hull on these heads if they were present. Our luck still held. We landed without losing a single LVT; not one of our men was injured. That luck was, however, being used up at a great rate.

As we were perhaps 150 feet from shore, a number of people came running down to the water's edge. I signaled to our LVT .50 and .30 caliber machine gunners to hold their fire when I saw the people were Marshallese and unarmed. They were waving frantically to us, as we found out later, to try to warn us of a coral ledge near the shore. The crowd included almost the entire population of the island. They thought our LVTs were boats and were going to wreck on the coral ledge. Their eyes were like saucers when they saw our cleated tracks bite into the ledge and our hulls heave up out of the water. They watched in awe as these rather clumsy amphibian vehicles loaded with marines crawled out of the water and up onto the beach. Fearing some kind of Japanese trap, our troops leaped over the sides of the seven-foot tall LVTs and fanned out into the bushes. Not a shot was fired.

Suddenly, having expected a fire fight, with dead and wounded, we had fifty or sixty grinning, wide-eyed friends, many of whom were carriers of gonorrhea. They termed gonorrhea "The American Disease." This naming was in honor of its donors. About one hundred years before our visit, American whaling ships were active in the mid-Pacific. The Marshallese had had visitors who preceded us in this exceptionally remote, tiny part of the earth.

The myth the people of Namorick had developed to explain their earlier American guests was fascinating in its creativity, given the minimal facts they had to work with. The white-sailed ships had only men in their crews. The ships made year-long voyages from the New England area where most of them were homeported. The crewmen, long celibate, were almost frantic for intercourse with the graceful, brown-skinned Marshallese women. They seemed superhuman in their possession of firearms, glass, navigation instruments, fabric sails, metals and insatiable libido.

The myth the Namorick people developed to explain all this was amazing in its theological inclusiveness: the Americans were some kind of demigods who came to the islands riding on white clouds which pushed their pau-paus (large canoes) through the water without the need for paddles. These demigods were strange creatures who had only one sex and that was male. They stayed in the clouds so much that their skins had turned white. They came to Namorick for the purpose of having sexual intercourse with the females, which was forbidden but wonderful to them and for which they would undertake exceedingly long and dangerous voyages. The American Disease was a God-given plague to punish them for their carnal joy in intercourse with creatures of lesser theological status.

When I heard this lovely, creative attempt to explain the unknown, I wondered about some of our own theological explanations. Though hardly a theological matter, I also wondered whether any of our men came down with a return gift.

Ebon Atoll: A Strange, Beautiful and Mysterious Place
When I first arrived at Ebon, I knew at once that I had never seen any place like it anywhere. The atoll was physically

different from any of the other Marshall Island atolls I had visited. The reef was more nearly circular and less elongated than Kwajalein. For whatever reason, almost all of the time I was there the reef was either above the level of the sea or, at the highest tide, barely beneath the water's surface. Perhaps because of these conditions, the lagoon was quite tranquil.

The lagoon itself seemed to communicate with the surrounding sea mostly through a narrow channel which ran between two closely-spaced islands. The current in this channel was surprisingly swift at maximum tide-change times. New LVTs could make about 6.2 knots at wide-open throttle. Ours were a long way from new and the better ones could not make six knots. I tried to run up this narrow channel at a time when the flow in it was less than its maximum of about two hours earlier. It took us nearly thirty minutes at full throttle to make two hundred to three hundred feet against the flow. We were able to make this snail-like progress only by running close to the almost vertical channel banks, where the current was a hair less than in midstream. My estimate was that the current was flowing at about five-and-a-half knots during our thirty-minute run. I had never seen anything even resembling these conditions in the wide, deep passes in the reef in other Marshall Island atolls. It was strange.

Another unusual feature of Ebon was the color of its vegetation. The coconut palm fronds were such a dark green that they appeared to be almost black. The trees were far taller and larger than the yellowish-green smaller palms characteristic of other atolls. Pandanus and breadfruit trees were luxurious in their growth. Their leaves were a rich, deep green. The entire atoll was strikingly beautiful.

Our earlier divided—and now much smaller—flotilla arrived at Ebon in the late afternoon. The sun was at our backs as we looked at the near islands, the channel I told you about, the lagoon, the far islands across the lagoon and the encircling reef. At a considerable distance from us, up on the reef and situated between two islands, was something we could not identify and about which we had no information. As usual, our intelligence was pitifully scanty. All we had in the way of maps were British naval charts dated 1854. They did not show anything unusual in the area in question. What we could see was à rounded object projecting several feet above the reef. It had what might be an embrasure or firing port, but this was sited in a direction less than appropriate for cannon fire aimed at protecting anything significant. Whatever it was, it was colored a bleached grayish-white, similar to that of a kind of Japanese hardened concrete used for fortifications.

A bit of intelligence information which we did have was that there was some kind of industrial activity at Ebon. This made no sense to us, except that they might be building coast defense emplacements. We could not conceive of any other type of industrial endeavor at a location so remote that it isn't even shown on some world atlas maps. If indeed this was a fortification, we could expect others, and better-placed ones at that. If correct, this spelled trouble, serious trouble, without our destroyers to level them before they could fire on us as we crawled over the reef in our assault. Despite intense concerns, we later received no fire from this unknown object.

Our wildest suppositions had not even come close to what we much later found this uncharted object to be. It was the sun-bleached hull of a wooden English trading ship which had foundered on the reef scores of years prior to our arrival. We wished for more non-threatening surprises.

We had orders to do everything possible to protect the Marshallese people, whom the Japs had treated exploitatively and brutally. To that end, we had an Australian man on board our ship who spoke some Marshallese. He was a courageous man, as were many of his countrymen. He was to leave our ship under cover of darkness in a tiny dinghy and make his way onto the nearby island, where it was believed most of the Marshallese people were located. He was to contact their chief and make arrangements for the native people to be protected as best this could be done.

For you, as you read this, possibly sitting in an easy chair with electric lights brightening your room, with dry clothes, no cuts or infections, a full belly, well-hydrated and with your greatest risk of massive, tearing bodily injury a possible traffic accident, it is difficult to imagine what this

Australian man faced. In the first place, the Japs had no illusions about what was going on. They had several warships lying off their atoll. It must have been quite clear that we had not come all that way as guests for a tea ceremony. They would expect us either to attack them in the dark or use that darkness to send in people to get tactical intelligence on the disposition of their forces. They would be on maximum alert to catch, torture, and kill anyone trying to sneak ashore.

Even before this one, however, there was perhaps another risk at least as great. We had no information on reef conditions, living coral beds, or offshore shallows. We were about four degrees north of the equator and perhaps 2000 to 4000 miles over open ocean from the nearest continent. The unobstructed Pacific has great, slow, heaving swells. These are often widely spaced, and they are of almost inconceivable power. I have seen them crush a twenty-foot-long, 33,000-pound LVT like a beer can run over by a bulldozer. The Aussie's tiny dinghy, to land at all, would have to be perfectly timed and expertly handled. Living coral can give a human horrendous cuts in which the toxic coral breaks off and lodges deep in the cut tissue. If you survive the immediate effects of the terrible cuts, you are almost certain to die of infection. We knew all this; our Australian brother-in-arms did too.

It was growing quite late in the afternoon as I stood on the stern deck of our LST with the Aussie. He realized that I had landed many times recently on somewhat similar reefs and was asking me well-put questions. I admired his bravery and was offering him anything and everything I knew, particularly about wave patterns and timing, something that we in the LVT battalions had found of life-saving importance. I was telling him how to watch for and recognize wave patterns so that he could try to use a pre-wave surge to boost his dinghy up on the reef. If he could do this, he might be able to avoid being crushed and cut to pieces on the coral. He and I both understood that he probably would be killed, if not by the sea, then by the Japs.

As we were speaking and as the sun drew lower in the west, we saw people launching a small vessel from a pocket in the reef that I had previously failed to notice. They were dressed in civilian clothes. Two of them boarded the vessel, which turned out to be an artfully-made pau-pau (canoe) with a single outrigger, sail and mast. A man sat on a tiny platform at the stern. He handled the tiller and the lines for trimming the sail. On a slightly larger, woven platform near the mast stood a tall, slim, elegant, dignified man with shoulder-length, gray-white hair. His skin was a deep color somewhere between copper and mahogany. His gaze was direct and level. There was no question who was the chief. He was dressed in a pressed, spotless, lace-trimmed, pink baby suit.

The Aussie and I stood staring as the helmsman brought his wee vessel alongside the stern of our gray steel warship.

The chief hailed us. The Aussie spoke back kindly in Marshallese. The chief and his helmsman showed an almost palpable relief. They had come with great courage, the chief to speak for his people, to do the best he could for them with a force infinitely greater than he, or they, could muster. The Aussie gave the chief specific instructions on where to hide his people after finding out from him how many he was responsible for and where they were located.

The sun was about to set. In the tropics there is only a short dusk, short indeed when only four degrees from the equator. The chief and his helmsman managed to sail back into their pocket in the reef just as darkness came on. We saw no muzzle flashes and heard no shots. We estimated that the pau-pau had made it back to shore. I wondered if our Australian comrade realized how a wholly unexpected event almost certainly had spared his life.

Our orders were to land on the main island of Ebon just after first light. We loaded marines into the LVTs on the enclosed tank deck of the LST. The vessel opened her bow doors and lowered her ramp. We drove down the ramp nose-first into the open sea just as faint light was dawning. We formed up and plowed toward the reef, firing our forward-mounted .50 caliber and .30 caliber machine guns in short bursts. We were so low in the water that we could fire with our muzzles parallel to the surface of the water and almost exactly at the level of the sand behind the beach. This fortunate circumstance allowed our tracer and armor-piercing bullets to skim over the ground surface in a manner deadly to defenders who were not well dug in.

Just before our hammering, tossing, bouncing climb out of the water and onto the reef, our .50 caliber gunner fired a short final burst. As he did so the heavy butt and receiver of his weapon, with powerful recoil, flew backward and hit him a damaging blow to the abdomen. This was somewhat similar to being kicked in the belly by a steel-shod mule. We were too tightly packed in the LVT for the gunner to fall to the deck. He doubled over in agony. The entire heavy weapon came back amongst our packed-in troops with its muzzle pointed toward some of them. There was surely a live round in the chamber of the .50 caliber piece. Without thinking or conscious intent, I grabbed the ammunition belt as it fed into the receiver of the gun and twisted it with all my strength. This jammed the feed so that if our gunner, in his agony, squeezed the trigger of the piece, it would not fire a great burst point-blank into the marines on board our LVT. Keeping the belt twisted, I grabbed the bolt handle and pulled it to the rear of the receiver. This cleared the live round from the chamber so that the piece could not fire.

My action took no more than a second or two. Our tracks began to claw into the soft coral rock of the reef. We began our heaving, tossing climb out of the water and onto the reef. You can be quite sure I kept that belt twisted so that the .50 caliber piece could not reload itself. Once the packed-in men had left, our gunner fell to the wet deck in agony. At that moment, I did not know what had happened and be-lieved that our man, his .50 caliber piece, or both, had been hit by enemy fire. I ordered our .30 caliber gunner to posi-tion his weapon so he could fire ahead of us or to each flank. I ordered our driver to keep our engine running and to be ready to move out if we were taken under fire. I then had time to see to our .50 caliber man.

I ripped off his dungaree jacket and looked for a wound. There was none. I pulled down his trousers. I could see no penetrating wound. I was confused. My expectation had precluded my recognizing other possibilities. He clearly was hurt and in great pain, but I could find no penetrating wound. I looked at his weapon. Things suddenly became clearer and possibly a bit better. The mounting bracket and rail had broken loose from the LVT hull from the recoil of the piece. Our man had taken some of this recoil in his ab-domen and sustained a blunt-trauma wound, with a pos-sible ruptured spleen, liver, pancreas or intestine. None of these could we see to on the beach. We had to get him, care-fully and gently, to the only medical care we had, that on our ship.

I ordered our co-driver to climb out of the tiny hatch leading from the cab to the open cargo compartment where the injured man and I were. I knew I would need his help in keeping our man from being thrown around as the LVT lurched and tossed upon re-entering the water on the way out to the ship. We did this and got the injured man back to the ship and hoisted aboard. In two years, no other instance of a broken .50 caliber mount had ever taken place. This was odd indeed. We returned to the beach, where I had the responsibility of directing other LVTs in bringing out wounded marines and bringing in ammunition, mortar shells, water and food.

We got back on the beach without incident and took up a position near its center. We had still received no enemy fire on the beach. There was a slack time for a few minutes, so I left the LVT to reconnoiter in case we had to move quickly. No more than forty to fifty feet from the beach was a thatched *fale*. At a glance, the workmanship was superb. It had a door facing me. There was hot, heavy gas and smoke coming from the door. As I peered in carefully from one side of the door, my weapon ready, I stood face-to-face with a stunning work of art. It was a life-size, charcoal-on-paper drawing of Jesus with a crown of thorns. His eyes looked directly into mine. They were slanted.

There was a loud "whoosh." The *fale* was enveloped in a fireball. I fell backwards with burning eyebrows. This was an experience so strange as to project me into an alternative reality.

There was no time to consider this discontinuity in my experience. A runner came back from the advancing marines to report that there were dead and wounded among them. It was essential to get an LVT up to them and then to our ship. As at Ailinglapalap, I was again faced with a situation requiring a difficult decision. That decision, at its best, was almost sure to be less than optimal. Again, I was the one best able to make the call on how to get at least one LVT up to the dead and wounded men. As before, if I went myself to find a practical route, I had to leave my post on the beach with several waiting LVTs. I put our platoon sergeant in charge of the LVTs on the beach, took the best running one of them and its crew to go along with me, and then set out on foot. There were no problems this time. We soon got to the wounded and hoisted them into the seven-foot-high vehicle. They needed to get the best care possible as soon as we could get them to the ship. I ordered our driver to follow his fresh tracks back to the beach and get the three wounded men to the LST. He was to order one of the LVTs waiting on the beach to come up to load our two dead marines and, in turn, take their bodies to the ship. We had to hurry with the wounded men; there was nothing we could do for our dead comrades other than to get them back to the ship and treat their bodies with respect on the way.

Our men had been killed and wounded by five Japanese Imperial Marines who had dug trap-door foxholes in a line ahead of two small buildings near the "industrial activity" area. These Imperial Marines were the best troops the Japs fielded. Every one I ever saw was six feet tall or taller. They routinely fought ferociously and to the death, taking as many of our people with them as they could. In this case, they had one man in each of five well-camouflaged, trap-door foxholes. Each had a rifle. As our men advanced toward them, having no hint of their presence, they simultaneously opened the lids of their foxholes and fired. They got off one round each before our people killed them. Each of their rounds hit one of our men, killing two and wounding three. I hated the yellow bastards, but I could not help admiring and being respectful of their skill and courage.

What were five of the absolute best fighting men the Japs had doing in this isolated place along with a few civilian workers? It made no sense. It was a mystery.

A further mystery was the "industrial activity" referred to in our intelligence briefing. I had some time between sending our wounded back and waiting for the other LVT to come up for the bodies of our two dead men. I began to look around. The "industrial area" was some kind of shallow surface mine. There were two small, open, steel railroad cars which sat on narrow gauge rails. There was no engine to pull the cars. The cars apparently were pushed by hand on rails that didn't seem to go to anything. Further, the entire island was only a few inches to a few feet above high tide level. You could dig only just a bit until you hit brackish water. The island itself was probably no more than a few hundred to a thousand acres in extent. You could scrape a few inches off the top of the whole thing and still not have much ore, if indeed there was any ore at all. Still further, I know of no mineable ores in the coral rock of the Marshall Islands. What in the world were the Japs doing here at Ebon with a few, a very few, of their best fighting men and a few Japanese civilians engaged in some kind of costly hand-mining of something of no known value in a place so remote that it is several thousand miles across open sea to anywhere there were people to use whatever it was that they were mining, if indeed there was any use at all for it?

This has been a persisting mystery to me, an irresolvable one. Perhaps one of you who reads this story has the answer.

Still More Strange Things at Ebon

I had specific orders prior to leaving Kwajalein on our reconnaissance to look for Amelia Earhart, her navigator, or evidence of their airplane. In the years before I was ordered to do this—and even more in the years after—the conspiracy theorists had a field day in speculating about what really happened to Earhart. I am confident that, at the time I received my orders, our military did not know what had happened to her and her navigator. As far as I am aware, we still do not. Despite questioning many people in the Marshalls and a great deal of looking, I found nothing.

While looking and asking at Ebon, I had two fascinating things happen. I have told you about trying to run against the current in the lagoon-to-sea channel. After running a long time against the current and making only a pitifully small distance, it was clear to me that we should moor our LVT and try to contact any Marshallese people we could find on the island. After some problems with swift current, we managed to get moored firmly, and one of our crew and I climbed ashore. I left two men in the LVT, both to guard it and to keep some slack in the mooring lines. Our crew and I were soon met by several Marshallese people, all men. I presumed there were women and children on the island, but that the men were keeping them out of sight to protect them.

The men were clearly friendly and glad to see us. There was one young man who was outstanding. He was a fine looking person, lighter-skinned than the others and with a faint waviness in his dark hair. He spoke just a bit of English. As time passed and I questioned him about Amelia Earhart and Fred Noonan, everyone began to be less tense and careful. The young man told me his name, clearly with the expectation that I would recognize it. I was confused. He smiled. In explanation and with honor, love and respect obvious in his voice, he said, "I am the son of Father Thomas Aquinas, our priest." I smiled back.

In our country today, I only wish that sons would honor, love, and respect their fathers as did this fine young man.

To try to add at least a bit of completeness to our search for evidence of our round-the-world fliers, I made a long trip across the lagoon to one of the far islands. It was much smaller than the name-island, Ebon. It was at least as beautiful, if not more so. It was indeed quite close to my picture of what a South Sea paradise might be. I wish that I could have stayed, at least for a while. We walked the ocean-side beach to look for any wreckage which might have been cast up by the sea. We found something, but not what we had been looking for. Partly buried in the coral sand was a solidly and carefully made, fair-sized wooden box. Years ago, such boxes were made to contain dynamite and were called "cases." They had closely-fitted, dovetail joints at each corner and were very sturdy.. The box we found had "U.S.S. Mississippi-flares" stenciled on it in black paint. Where had it floated from? One can only guess.

I have always wanted to go back to this strange and lovely place.

So ended our reconnaissance, our mission accomplished, and not a man in our Lost Company killed in action—truly a success, as well as an unforgettable life experience.

Time of Decision: Point of No Return

SINCE THE TIME of the founding of our nation, people from Philadelphia have been important in the Marine Corps. Many have served their country well.

So it was with "Skipper." As the eldest son of an immensely influential old Philadelphia family, he literally lived on the Main Line. He had gone to the best prep school and to a fine university.

Several days after entering Officers' Candidate School— where I met him, and he was in my class—he had been married to an attractive young lady of similar family status whom he had known since childhood. She had made her debut after going to finishing school. Her family and his family mated them in a Middle Atlantic States equivalent to a royal family's arranged marriage.

In the frenzy of mobilization in the first months of World War II, many formalities of usual living had to be dispensed with. Skipper's bride lived with her family in their home until he could secure a one-room "apartment" for the two of them near our Quantico training base.

Skipper introduced me to this young lady at a social function. I talked with her for a few minutes and found her to be a blond, fair-skinned, conventional person who had seen little of the hard side of life. She seemed capable of having babies with the expert help of well-trained obstetricians. She was pleasant, pretty, and skilled socially.

The two of them lived together for a couple of months in the midst of our frenetic, consuming and dangerous training. I was so exhausted at night that all I could relate to was a bath, a meal, dry clothes and sleep. I can't imagine that Skipper had much left over for the slow and personally demanding development of real intimacy with her. Both seemed fairly well satisfied with what probably was a rather superficial and cool relationship.

Though I liked Skipper and respected his obvious courage and dedication to his training for the awful duty that we knew was coming, I had little contact with the twosome. She did not follow Skipper to the West Coast, where we went for further training.

We arrived in California at Camp Pendleton after the delivery of only a few of our newer model landing vehicles. Not long after we got there and after we had received some more of the new LVTs, the assault on Tarawa took place with its terrible casualties.

The word we had was that many of our marines were killed trying to wade across the wide coral reef. One of our brother LVT battalions had been only partly equipped with the tank-like, but open-topped, vehicles which were capable of climbing out of the sea, mounting the reef and then traversing it to reach the beach and deliver the riflemen they carried. There had been only enough LVTs to mount the first couple of waves of troops. The following battalions of marines were loaded into small boats. These could not deliver the men any farther than the edge of the reef. They left the boats only to have to wade, knee-deep, across the several hundred feet of reef under murderous Japanese fire. The losses were horrendous. It was clear that we had to adapt our tactics if any of us were going to survive.

Suddenly, our LVT battalions were far more important than they had previously been considered. We began getting more new LVTs. Our under-strength rosters began to fill. New LVT battalions were split off from the original ones. Various people were promoted. Skipper was one of those. He was made a company commander in our old battalion, and I was placed in one of the new ones. We kept in touch though—all of us, both men and officers. We had all started out together and felt a growing bond after having worked together for a time.

Our whole operations changed almost overnight. We had to work out ways to load LVTs into tank landing ships so that the troops and the LVTs could go together on the same vessel to the shore being attacked. We loaded the riflemen, mortar men, flame thrower teams and other troops directly into the LVTs while still in the tank deck of the ships. The ship's forward doors then opened, its ramp was lowered, and the loaded LVTs went under their own power down the ramp and directly into the sea. The LVTs then carried their men across the open sea, across the reef and onto the beach.

This all may seem simple in its telling, but it was immensely harder than that to develop and implement. Skipper and I were in the midst of this development and worked together on numerous occasions. I came to know him better and to have deepening respect for his decisiveness and responsibility. Oddly, I heard him mention his wife only once or twice in a period of many weeks. As best I can remember, she never made it from Philadelphia to Oceanside, California, despite our being there for months. Skipper's married fellow officers managed to have their wives join them before our final departure for the assault at Kwajalein. This was not due to Skipper's lack of funds; his family and her family could have bought part of the West Coast, if necessary. I wondered if his attitude was one more of disinterest than of distaste.

We combat-loaded out of San Diego for the soon-to-be fighting in the Marshall Islands. The Japanese had been awarded the Marshalls in the settlement after World War I. They were known to have been fortifying them in the intervening years between World War I and World War II. As best I could interpret the little intelligence information that filtered down to my level, the operation was going to be risky at best. Our support in the Hawaiian Islands was thousands of miles to the east. We had no land-protected waters, no bay or estuary to protect us from the open sea in the disgorgement in our fragile LVTs. You can scarcely imagine the enormity of the immense Pacific swells when viewed from six inches of freeboard above the surface, which was all we had when our twenty-man load, with arms and ammunition, was aboard.

In addition, our orders were to land in the initial assault on the seaward side of a small island situated down the reef from the main islands of Roi and Namur. This presented major problems, since the reef at that point was razor-sharp, living coral. Onto that coral rushed twelve-foot, open-ocean swells. I could feel the shock waves produced by the sea waves on the coral. They came through the water to the tin-can-thick hull of my LVT with an impact that bespoke their enormous power.

I led the first wave of LVTs. I had to decide whether to attempt a crawl-out with a timing between swells, possibly too short to allow it, or to invent something else. I ordered our driver to pause for a minute so I could try to time the swells in my mind. We laid to and rolled sickeningly and perilously as I timed the crest-to-crest period. It was too short; a catastrophe was certain if I ordered us to land on the open-sea reef. We would have been upended and sunk by the next swell before we could climb out of the trough and onto the reef. After being cast out on the reef, any survivors would have been cut to pieces by the coral.

As I contemplated this horror as compared to the one, if I survived, of running into a mine field on the lagoon side of the island, one of the marines jammed in next to me vomited his K ration chocolate and dried fruit bar. I caught it in the face and chest. Somehow, this made up my mind. I signaled the rest of the LVTs and moved through a deep-water pass at the end of the island and into the calm waters of the lagoon. We landed on the coral sand beach, all of us, without setting off a single mine. Skipper followed me in with his wave of LVTs without a loss.

My thankfulness was so great that I was about to begin a gasping kind of sobbing when that damned Skipper came up to me and started laughing at my vomit-coated face and chest. One of my men told Skipper, "It isn't even his own." There was a great chorus of laughter. I walked out knee-deep in the water of the lagoon and washed off the big lumps and most of the rest. I wanted to kill Skipper, but in the midst of my walking toward him with homicidal intent, I started to laugh myself. This was easier, because the vomiter had not had the chocolate and fruit bar down long enough for it to get sour. After laughing a while and giving Skipper the finger, I resumed command and got my LVTs together for a run to the ship to reload and carry more troops ashore.

I tell you this to give you some idea of the emotional depth of the bonds that are forged over the years between men living, and surviving, in the awful circumstances which we did. It may help you to understand what follows.

Later, all of us in the LVT battalions had been badly shot

up in the Marianas Islands and at Iwo. Skipper had lost many of his men, and he grieved for them. He had been hit as well, but never left his command. His flesh wound was dressed at an aid station, and he was never hospitalized. He and most of the rest of us began to get "burned out," a kind of dulling of sensibilities and an uncaringness. We returned to the Hawaiian Islands for rest, for replacement of our lost men with green recruits, and for re-equipment with a new model LVT.

Skipper seemed especially stressed. I saw him in a telephone booth on several occasions when we went into the nearby little town where we sometimes walked in the evening. Though I understood it not at all, Skipper would be in the booth for an hour or more at a time. In that day, overseas telephone calls were by underseas cable or by radio. They took a long time to make, and the expense was beyond my imagination.

Skipper was making calls to his wife and family to tell them he had decided to get divorced. The reaction from stateside was intense. I had never had any personal experience with immensely wealthy, powerful, and politically dominant families. I was dumbfounded. Our colonel began getting overseas calls from Skipper's family, from his wife's family, and from highly-placed persons. He had to take calls from a senator, the State Department and from the commandant of the Marine Corps.

To add to all this, Skipper had met at the Navy Club the

single most physically beautiful woman I have ever known. She was so beautiful that it was frightening when I met her. This girl, probably about 23 or 24 years old, was perfectly formed but tiny, probably four feet ten or eleven inches tall, with jet-black hair hanging nearly to her waist. Her skin was deep tan and perfect, without a blemish of any kind. She was part Chinese, part Hawaiian and part Portuguese. Her dark eyes sparkled with life and fire.

For many men the power of their person and their dominance arises in part out of physical size, when their bodies are well-formed and not distorted. With many women, it seems to me the opposite. Their personal presence and personal power—in Samoan, their *Mana*—are inversely related to their physical size. This was the case with Taia. Her presence was compelling. She was regal, yet at the same time sparkling, perhaps like a tiny, perfectly-cut jewel.

Strangely, Taia had grown up unspoiled. She had none of the petulant, demanding, baby-dollism I had known and despised in beautiful Southern women. Taia was pleasant, friendly, non status-conscious. But most of all, she was vital; she exuded life. I had never met anyone like her, and neither had Skipper.

He was smitten, and so was she. They were clearly taken with each other. Their relationship developed quickly and was so intense that it could have been disastrous.

Skipper had been wounded and overseas so long that he could opt for discharge from the Marine Corps. This he did. In addition, he completed his divorce. More hell came from stateside. Our colonel was in a bad spot. Skipper was perfectly competent, he had the points, he could be discharged if he wished. His divorce was uncontested, swift, and expensive.

Still, it took time. During that time, the atomic bombs were dropped and formal hostilities with the Japanese ended. Our LVT battalions got the word to strike camp, pack our gear and board ship for return to the States.

For a couple of days, we loaded aboard an LST moored to the small dock at Kahului, Maui, a few miles from our now struck camp at Maalea Bay. Skipper, by then discharged from the Marine Corps and living with Taia in Kahului, got word that we were ready to depart.

Our men jammed the vessel's deck. We were looking forward to resuming our lives in the States, with all that meant. Skipper came down to say goodbye. We and Skipper had bonds formed in fire and death; those are deep in brothers-in-arms. It was painful. Skipper had Taia with him. Our ship slipped her moorings, sounded her horn in a great blast, and started to move away from the dock.

Skipper waved goodbye. We waved. He and Taia turned and walked away. Skipper never looked back. He had decided.

About the Author

GEORGE SCIPLE WAS born in Atlanta, Georgia on March 1, 1921. He grew up as a child of the Great Depression.

His father had a large and growing business. The chaotic economic circumstances of the onset of the Depression suddenly forced him into bankruptcy. The family went within a short time from having whatever they might want to having little to eat.

His father had a cardiac arrest during a surgical procedure and barely survived. He was extensively disabled thereafter.

The family moved in with his grandmother, who had not long before been widowed. Things were grim.

George was admitted to Emory University after completing grammar and high schools in the public schools. He did well academically at Emory and was elected to the Phi Beta Kappa honor society.

George enlisted in the U.S. Marine Corps Reserve shortly after the Japanese attacked Pearl Harbor. He was in his senior year at Emory at this time and was allowed to continue in school for several months to complete his degree before being called to active duty.

His father's business had been associated with automotive equipment and internal combustion engines, and George had absorbed a good deal of information and had some bit of experience in this area. This stood him in good stead when he was assigned to Landing Vehicle School and later to an LVT battalion in Fleet Marine Force.

His overseas service was entirely in the Pacific area in WW II. After the end of hostilities, and using the benefits of the G.I. Bill, he was able to complete the work and graduate from Emory University Medical School.

He lives with Marjorie, his wife of more than fifty years, in Brunswick, Georgia.

Breinigsville, PA USA
13 January 2011
253174BV00002B/253/A

9 781878 853783